DON'T TRY THIS ALONE

HOW TO BUILD DEEP COMMUNITY WHEN YOU WANT TO HIDE FROM YOUR PAIN

Toni Collier

FOUNDER OF **BROKEN CRAYONS STILL COLOR**

An Imprint of Thomas Nelson

Don't Try This Alone

Copyright © 2025 by Toni J. Collier

All rights reserved. No portion of this book may be reproduced, stored in a retrieval system, or transmitted in any form or by any means—electronic, mechanical, photocopy, recording, scanning, or other—except for brief quotations in critical reviews or articles, without the prior written permission of the publisher.

Published in Nashville, Tennessee, by Nelson Books, an imprint of Thomas Nelson. Nelson Books and Thomas Nelson are registered trademarks of HarperCollins Christian Publishing, Inc.

The author is represented by Alive Literary Agency, www.aliveliterary.com.

Thomas Nelson titles may be purchased in bulk for educational, business, fundraising, or sales promotional use. For information, please email SpecialMarkets@ThomasNelson.com.

Unless otherwise noted, Scripture quotations are taken from the Holy Bible, New International Version®, NIV®. Copyright © 1973, 1978, 1984, 2011 by Biblica, Inc.® Used by permission of Zondervan. All rights reserved worldwide. www.zondervan.com. The "NIV" and "New International Version" are trademarks registered in the United States Patent and Trademark Office by Biblica, Inc.® Scripture quotations marked CSB are taken from the Christian Standard Bible®. Copyright © 2017 by Holman Bible Publishers. Used by permission. Christian Standard Bible® and CSB® are federally registered trademarks of Holman Bible Publishers. Scripture quotations marked KJV are taken from the King James Version. Public domain. Scripture quotations marked MSG are taken from *The Message*. Copyright © 1993, 2002, 2018 by Eugene H. Peterson. Used by permission of NavPress. All rights reserved. Represented by Tyndale House Publishers, Inc.

Names and identifying characteristics of some individuals have been changed to preserve their privacy.

Any internet addresses, phone numbers, or company or product information printed in this book are offered as a resource and are not intended in any way to be or to imply an endorsement by Thomas Nelson, nor does Thomas Nelson vouch for the existence, content, or services of these sites, phone numbers, companies, or products beyond the life of this book.

Library of Congress Cataloging-in-Publication Data

Names: Collier, Toni J., 1991– author.
Title: Don't try this alone : how to build deep community when you want to hide from your pain / Toni Collier.
Description: Nashville, Tennessee : Nelson Books, 2025. | Summary: "Author and founder of Broken Crayons Still Color, Toni Collier shows readers that it's not only possible to heal from the things that have broken you but that you can build a strong, life-giving community to support you, be with you in the valleys, and speak love and truth into your life as God puts you back together again"— Provided by publisher.
Identifiers: LCCN 2025001105 (print) | LCCN 2025001106 (ebook) | ISBN 9781400233540 (hardcover) | ISBN 9781400254309 (ITPE) | ISBN 9781400233557 (ebook)
Subjects: LCSH: Fellowship—Religious aspects—Christianity. | Communities—Religious aspects—Christianity. | Friendship—Religious aspects—Christianity. | Healing—Religious aspects—Christianity.
Classification: LCC BV4517.5 .C65 2025 (print) | LCC BV4517.5 (ebook) | DDC 248.4—dc23/eng/20250403
LC record available at https://lccn.loc.gov/2025001105
LC ebook record available at https://lccn.loc.gov/2025001106

Printed in the United States of America
25 26 27 28 29 LBC 5 4 3 2 1

To my confessional community, my Thirty-Ayyyeee gals, and every single person in my village. *You know who you are.* Thank you. I haven't seen a year of my life as hard as the one I lived starting September 2023. I've never cried so hard, slept and ate so little, and prayed so fervently—and there you all were. Wiping every tear, buying furniture for my house, making sure I got to the gym, praying for me, protecting me, and believing me. I would not have survived the valleys without you—I owe you this book and the healing I would not have accessed without you.

To Anna Julia, my au pair and sister. Thank you for helping me raise my children. This book would not have been completed without your support and love for our family. Thank you for staying and praying and helping and dancing with us through the hard moments.

And to my parents, thank you for teaching me to stop on the side of the road to help strangers, to open my house to whoever would accept the invite, and to always choose a generous life. You taught me how to build, love, and be family. Your seeds were the reason for this book and my community. Thank you a million times. I love you both.

To my children, Dyl and Sammie. I never gave up.

CONTENTS

Foreword by Jackie Hill Perry vii
Introduction (Don't Skip This) xi

Chapter 1 You Were Created for Withness 1

Part 1: Why You Try to Heal Alone 13

Chapter 2 You Don't Feel Seen, Soothed, Safe, or Secure . . 15
Chapter 3 Your Shame Keeps You Isolated 29
Chapter 4 You're Afraid of Being Found 42
Chapter 5 You've Been Hurt by the Responses of Those
             Close to You 54
Chapter 6 You Struggle to Believe That God Never
             Leaves You 65

Part 2: How to Build a Strong Community 75

Chapter 7 Understand Adult Friendship 77
Chapter 8 Look for the Characteristics of a Good Friend . . 93
Chapter 9 Find the Right Players for Your Team 108
Chapter 10 Embrace Diversity 124

CONTENTS

Chapter 11 Create Your Own Confessional Community . . . 138

Part 3: What to Remember on Your Healing Journey . . 151

Chapter 12 Remember That God Is in Control 153
Chapter 13 Remember to Ask Your Community to Help
Carry Your Burdens 165
Chapter 14 Remember That God Can Use Strangers 178
Chapter 15 Remember to Be a Good Friend When
Someone Else Is in Pain 194

Conclusion 209
Acknowledgments 215
Notes 217
About the Author 219

FOREWORD

It feels hypocritical to write the foreword to a book like *this* one. Maybe if the subject was something like the hypostatic union, I would carry some degree of insecurity but at least I could write without fear. Intellectualism is easy. Relationships are not. And I know this theologically of course. One only has to read three chapters into the Bible to see the breakdown of this thing we call "community," with what started as two people naked and unashamed becoming two people, then two more, then an entire world addicted to themselves. Because of this, nobody loves anybody consistently. Everyone is selfish. Everyone is anxious. Everyone is insecure and projects meaning onto ambiguity even if the narrative is shaped by trauma and not reality.

I am a native to relational suffering, hence my resistance to being at ease when writing a foreword to a book like this one. Toni doesn't want us to do it alone, but what happens when isolation feels like a refuge? Like wisdom, even? What happens when the monster under the bed manifests in the leader over you? Who can rest in any relationship when your nightmares keep coming true?

FOREWORD

I suspect you're discerning that I've been through some things that have made me a smidge cynical. Maybe you picked up this book because you are too. If so, we are alike in this way. Moving about the world with a wounded heart and a soft conscience that knows life is not life without people in it. People who can see the you that you are hiding from. The part of you that died when you were betrayed. That part of you that loves to be loved and is simply tired of disappointment feeling familiar.

With that in mind, if any humility exists, we must also admit that we have not lived on one side of the pendulum our entire lives. Judas might've kissed you once or twice, but there might be someone somewhere who, after a moment with you, is still wiping their cheek. And that's the thing with people. We are not God nor naturally godly, and therefore the pain is often mutual. Yet the sometimes-irritating irony of it all is that none of us can be healed or holy without people. So to overcome what has broken us, we need people. To overcome what is hindering us, we need people. There is no other way to exist in God's world faithfully than alongside another image bearer.

All of this scares me, and that fear has kept me not only from people but from God Himself. Alone in that room, you might feel safe, but you are also suffocating. In that disappointment or pain it might feel risky to let someone see how weak you can be. Having that set of temptations and confessing how beautiful you want to believe a lie is doesn't seem wise to share. But what if God wanted to meet you through His people? What if the church (the invisible Church) is an actual temple of the Holy Spirit, and by inviting other Christians into your world you are creating space to experience what God has to offer you *through* them?

Remember Paul who testified that God was the "source of all comfort"? We know this to be the case, and it can tempt us to believe that being in our prayer closet, alone with Christ, is the *only* way to look to the hills from which our help comes from. But understand this: the Lord is our ultimate source *and* He has decided to set His church apart as a *conduit* of His comfort: "Blessed be the God and Father of our Lord Jesus Christ, the Father of mercies and the God of all comfort. He comforts us in all our affliction, so that we may be able to comfort those who are in any kind of affliction, through the comfort we ourselves receive from God. For just as the sufferings of Christ overflow to us, so also through Christ our comfort overflows" (2 Corinthians 1:3–5 CSB).

I believe this book is God's comfort coming for you. Through another person. A fellow image bearer who knows what pain is. Toni has walked through the valley and seen the shadow of death and has decided to fear no evil. She has experienced God's rod and staff and how the mechanism of His comfort and correction is by way of flesh and bones. She knows what hurt is and how the healing we all want is on the other side of not trying anything alone. Watch the way God meets you through the words of someone else so that when the chapters end and the book is closed, this work will testify that it never was and never will be good for man to be alone.

Jackie Hill Perry

INTRODUCTION

(Don't Skip This)

"My marriage is over, right? I have to leave, right?"

My friend Jamie held me in her arms in the hallway of the Conrad Hotel in Nashville as devastation set in.

The bad thing had happened. I was crushed—or so I thought.

At 6:00 a.m. I'd woken up to a phone call from my now ex-husband to hear the worst possible news about my marriage. It had happened again. Apologies again. Betrayal again. I just remember staring at the phone, completely numb with so many thoughts running through my head.

- **Disgust.** *How could anyone do this to someone they love, the family they love, the children they love, to God? What about everything we've built? What about our house? What about our future? Our grandkids that haven't been born yet?*
- **Disbelief.** *No. This isn't happening again. I don't*

believe it. I'm asleep and this is a nightmare. Wake up, Toni, wake up!
- **Despair.** *I can't make it through another trauma. I've already been through too much. This will crush me. I won't be strong enough for my children. How will I raise them? I can't handle any more pain.*
- **Disappointment.** *I'm not mad, but I feel disappointed that this is actually the reality of my life, that God would allow this.*

My shoulders were slumped and my eyes glazed over when I'd gotten off the phone. No emotion. I'd ended the call by saying, "Thanks for telling me. I'm going to go process this in a safe space. I hope you get the help you need."

Thankfully two of my closest friends were staying in the Conrad Hotel on the same floor as me: Jamie and Jessica, who had both been walking deeply with me in a group called a confessional community (we'll talk about that in more detail later). The previous day we had filmed a show, together with my friend Lisa, on a Christian network. They were just a few rooms down the hall.

God knew I would need them.

My hands were shaking when I texted them.

Hey, are you guys up? I have a very private emergency. I'm sorry to bother you this early.

They both joined a FaceTime with me immediately, and I told them everything. I cried. I was so afraid. They were right there.

INTRODUCTION

After we got off the phone, both of them texted me reassuring words:

> **Jamie:** We *love you dearly* and are in your corner and fighting for you. It's okay to be needy. *The Lord is your strength* right now. We can talk whenever you want.
>
> **Jessica:** Love you. You aren't alone today or tomorrow or the next day. You aren't who you were, and you didn't have the resources (emotional, communal, financial) that you have now.

They came for me just like Jesus would. I needed safe people, and they met my need. I needed people who would just listen, and they listened. I needed my people when it felt like the pain was on the edge of crushing me.

And if I've discovered anything as I've walked through this season, it's that you probably need people too.

Why I Wrote This Book

This wasn't the book I was supposed to write. I'd just turned in a fifty-thousand-word manuscript for a book on sanctification (which is just a fancy word for living a life honoring and pleasing to God after you say yes to Jesus). I was honest and raw about my personal sin and how dark my past had been in hopes that readers would feel less alone in their own past sin and turn to the God who cleanses all things—who hasn't given up on us, ever. After turning the book in, I was so relieved. I even celebrated with my friends with a little sushi night. All that was left were edits and to actually release the book into the world.

Then I was headed toward my second divorce.

I started feeling like that book wasn't the book I was supposed to release. I'd been through so much pain at the hand of someone else's sin that I didn't want to market, release, tour, and talk about sin in that way. I wasn't ready, and my publisher agreed that after going through a public divorce, it wasn't wise. Even though I believe God's timing and promptings are right and good, this one really sucked.

I was devastated—and then something beautiful happened. I told my confessional community group about not releasing that book during one of our monthly calls. They had already witnessed tears flow from heartbreak, sadness, and anxiety—now they were holding disappointment with me.

"Aww, Toni," Jessica said, "I'm so sorry. After all the work you put into it, that really does suck. I'm disappointed with you."

Jennie agreed. "That book is for later. It will come out one day."

"Toni, I wish I could just fly myself down to Atlanta and give you a big hug," Ann whispered. "I'm deeply sorry."

"Love you, T," Lindsey added.

And then Jamie said something that changed the direction of the conversation. She took herself off mute and jokingly said, "I was serious when I messaged you on Instagram that what you posted should be your next book! I think it would be a really good one."

INTRODUCTION

I had posted about and tagged almost every person who helped me and my kids while I was navigating and healing from divorce, figuring out finances, managing a public platform, caring for my au pair who moved from Brazil to live with me and help me with my children, finding a new place to live, and much more. I was so grateful, and I needed to share that because of God and His people, I more than survived—I thrived. The last slide in a series of Instagram posts held these three words: *Don't heal alone.*

Those were the words Jamie was talking about, and everyone on our confessional community call lit up. They all believed with me that this topic would indeed be my next book. And that, my friend, is the power of not doing life alone. That is why you are here reading this book today.

Community turns dark and weighty things into easier victories. So welcome to the victory that my beautiful group of baddies (that's what we call each other in the confessional community) helped me reach. Welcome to the book God knew I was supposed to write—for me, for many around the world, and for you. I'm so glad that it's not by coincidence that you're reading *Don't Try This Alone.*

You Aren't Alone

Reading this book isn't going to be easy. Surprise! The healing journey is never easy, and it'll never be a straight path. It's messy and heavy and can feel crushing. We need assistance. We need a coach. I'm offering to be your bestie don't-heal-alone coach:

INTRODUCTION

- I'll always be honest and vulnerable about my difficult journey with pain, betrayal, and disappointment.
- I'll openly share any resources that have helped me heal.
- I'll be honest about my weaknesses and how my friends and family helped to strengthen me—there was no way I could do this alone.
- I'll always bring God's truth to the table.
- I'll challenge you to do and say the hard things required to build a healthy community that is not only there to help but able to hold you accountable.
- I'll make sure we laugh a little and take breaks so that we can get through this together. After all, hope and hurt can coexist.

But before we get started, here are two things you need to know:

1. **What it will cost you.** (Ouch—I know.) You can't hide anymore. You've got to step into the light, okay? You have to get out of the darkness of your hidden pain and start sharing openly. You're going to have to trust again if you've been hurt. And I'm sorry for that. You'll have to trust God with your heart—all of it. You'll have hard conversations with people who may not be ready to stand with you in the trenches. You'll have new boundaries in relationships that may make you sad. You'll have to tell your people about the pain you're going through again and again—this may sting.

2. **What you'll gain.** You'll beat the mess out of shame. You'll find people who are trustworthy, and you'll start feeling safer in your body and in this broken world. God will meet you and blow your mind. He'll send people your way that just get it, He'll comfort you when it's scary, and He'll heal you.

   You'll learn that boundaries are biblical and a way to honor your own heart. You'll experience feeling seen in really intentional ways when you call a friend and they let you cry for as long as you need with no words spoken. They'll listen to you tell "the story" a million times until you feel better. Your healing journey will be easier, and your people will be there to witness it.

I'm hopeful for you. I believe in your resilience to do hard things. I don't think you'd pick up a book on healing with others if you weren't serious about your healing journey. You are such an overcomer. Every tear that you've cried is stunning.

You're going to make it. And this book will help you do just that. Healing with people by your side won't be easy, but you were made for it, and you will do it. I know it.

I believe in these words that you're reading because I've seen it through my own pain and know with every fiber of my being that if you lean into this concept of not healing alone, you will look back on the dark moments and remember where the light pierced through.

You'll see the goodness of God in the land of the living (Psalm 27:13). The dry rocks in your life will be pierced open,

INTRODUCTION

and you won't be left thirsty—you have access to living water (John 4:13–14). When you're out of this valley, you and God and your people will rejoice because you made it to the other side. You'll rejoice because pain didn't crush you—because you didn't face it alone. As you go through this book, whether it's by yourself or with a close friend, book club, or small group, remember those truths as you dive in.

Here's what our journey together will look like: In the first part of the book, I address the reasons we try to heal alone. If we're going to fix anything, we've got to know where our brokenness comes from in the first place. The truth is we want to heal alone for so many reasons—we're ashamed, we've been taught to numb and hide, or we're afraid and have good reason to be. Once we address those things and willingly name them, we'll be able to start healing them so we can move on to the next section of this book—the practical stuff (my favorite!).

In part 2 we will talk about how to *actually* build your community. Because let's be honest: It can be weird finding new friends—especially as an adult. We'll get practical and dive into what to look for, red flags to be aware of, and how to navigate friendships in need of transition. All the things.

Last, in part 3, we'll fill your "community backpack" with ways to sustain the community you have built. We'll even take a moment to figure out how you can be community for others. After all, relationships aren't one-sided. And if we want healthy, God-fearing, reliable friends who help us heal, we will have to be healthy, God-fearing, reliable friends who help others heal too.

Let's dive right on in.

Chapter 1

YOU WERE CREATED FOR WITHNESS

Have you ever felt like your pain would crush you? Maybe it's a long-term pain that feels like it'll never let up. Maybe you're going through a season of singleness that feels like it'll never end. You've followed the rules, you've honored God with your body, and you've focused on your mental and emotional health. You've even attended all the singles' events, but it just doesn't seem that God is being intentional about sending your spouse.

Or perhaps it's a challenging kid. Been there, and I've got all the battle scars to prove it. You've tried gentle parenting, made mistakes with that, and slipped into aggressive parenting instead. *No judgment here.* You went and got the diagnosis, tried different dosages of medication, promised candy if the behavioral chart had more green colors than red ones. You may have cried uncontrollably in front of your tiny human because all their behaviors triggered all your inadequacies. It seems they'll never learn to regulate, they'll never be on the honor roll, and you'll always feel mom guilt for taking your own sadness out on them.

Maybe it's not being a parent that has caused your pain, but being the child. The pain of abandonment by a father who selfishly chose not to be present for you. Or here's a taboo topic—motherhood wounds. Maybe it's pain from the mother who kept choosing her addiction over your tiny, fragile heart.

Or perhaps it's the longing in your heart to be a better parent than the ones you had, or just to be a parent at all. There's the pain of infertility or miscarriage, and the longing you have to hold your very own tiny human keeps you up at night. You're pleading and asking God to please return what was lost—or at least give you what you don't have at all.

These long-term, painful, broken parts of our stories get more excruciating with time. I know the pain of something not getting better. And I know what it feels like to have the same trauma and pain revisit over and over again, poking and prodding and peeling. I know that in-between space where you think, *This really sucks*, and *I'm not surprised*.

But maybe for you it wasn't a long-term familiar pain—it was sudden. You received that diagnosis, and in one moment your healthy turned into "How long do I have?" or "Is there a cure?" Maybe it was you, sweet friend, who were unfaithful, and the person you once trusted to keep your secret spilled the beans. Now the look in your spouse's eyes is permanently seared into your brain.

And the grief of losing someone suddenly is like getting your pants pocket stuck on the handle of a door—there's a jolt that brings you into shock and disbelief. Your mother, no longer with you or able to remind you if it's a tablespoon or teaspoon of salt needed in her favorite recipe. Your father can no longer hop on a FaceTime to help you fix the flat tire that happened when you were on the way to something important.

That sudden pain knocks the wind out of you. Makes surprises feel cruel. Turns birthdays and holidays and anniversaries into memorials instead of celebrations. Sucks you into sadness like a garbage disposal.

And no matter how quick or slow or short or long the pain is, it rushes in and turns into unwelcome chills down your body, into nausea that turns into sleepless nights into despair. And every single one of your bones is aching, and they won't stop. It's like your organs are being twisted and turned. All you want is for the pain to stop. To stop hurting. To stop ruining and crushing and taking.

Pain is a violent thief, isn't it?

Okay, let's take a break. If I were sitting in a coffee shop with you as this conversation is flowing, I would give us a break right here. And I would say I'm sorry. I'm so sorry for whatever pain took from you. I'm so deeply sorry. And I feel seen because it took so much from me too. I'm reminded of Jessica's words: "You aren't alone today or tomorrow or the next day." This is the healing balm that held my arms up, because we were designed to have our arms held up when life gets too heavy to do it ourselves. So take a deep breath right here. Really deep. Now hold it and then blow out for longer than you breathed in. Do that three times.

And then let's dive back in. When you're ready and not before, okay?

———

Sometimes anticipating pain can be more crushing than the pain itself.

For people like me, who have lived through really hard things—sexual manipulation and abuse, addiction, an eating disorder, two divorces—it's extremely difficult for me to believe that something bad isn't always around the corner.

I want to be more optimistic. I want to believe that there's good coming my way, but I'm also so scared that it's just *not*. I live in this constant tension, fighting to believe that a good God will come for me and protect me from evil, and knowing the reality that we live in a fallen, broken world and evil is on its way too.

Here's an uncomfortable truth: We can follow God and still experience hard and painful things. The Israelites are a perfect example of this.

In the Bible the Israelites were following Moses from Egypt

*You aren't
alone today or
tomorrow
or the next day.*

to Canaan. They camped in a place called Rephidim, "but there was no water for the people to drink. So they quarreled with Moses" (Exodus 17:1–2). I want to point out that these people left behind bondage and all they had known to follow God's plan for their lives. They were following the will of God, but that did not come with protection from imperfection or pain.

Moses knew that even when pain and longing come into our hearts, our God is able to fulfill those longings and provide a way forward. Moses did what we see him do best—he took his difficulties to the Lord. And look at what God's first instruction was: "The LORD answered Moses, 'Go out in front of the people. Take with you some of the elders of Israel and take in your hand the staff with which you struck the Nile, and go. I will stand there before you by the rock at Horeb'" (Exodus 17:5–6).

God's way forward through hard things will always be with Him and His people. God knew exactly what Moses needed to provide for the Israelites: He needed the God of divine presence, and he needed the physical, tangible presence of God's people (the elders of Israel) if he was going to lead these people out of bondage, through the impossible, and onward to a peaceful place. Moses knew that the only way beyond the pain is through the pain. And he was reminded by God that he couldn't—or maybe shouldn't—do it alone.

The next part of the story gets a little weird. God told Moses to "strike the rock, and water will come out of it for the people to drink" (v. 6). Um, what? Strike a rock and water is just going to miraculously come out? Moses and the whole group of people knew that this wasn't normal. This is not how you get water; water then was typically obtained from a well, spring, or bag made from sheepskin. Hitting a rock doesn't get you water. But in this miraculously generous act of God, it did. Moses wasn't the only one to witness it; the elders and almost two million Israelites did too. Moses believed in God in the midst of a real need, and because of his surrender to God's presence and His people, everyone around him got to experience the miracle.

The Miracle of Presence

Reminders of God's presence and the importance of living in witness are found outside the Bible too. I had a reminder of this recently during a hard day. It was a grief day for me. I cried after dropping my daughter off to school. I cried on the way home from the gym. I cried as I went to work, leaving my son with my au pair, Anna Julia. I cried on social media, allowing people to see the raw and honest reality of healing from divorce after betrayal. Seven months after having to leave my marriage, there was still grief. Staring me in the face was the very thing I didn't want to happen.

On my Instagram Stories I said, "It just sucks, you know? I have my moments when I don't want to have to endure so much. I don't want to be broken." That's a wild statement from the girl who founded an organization called Broken Crayons Still Color. And also, it's just the truth.

But guess what happened at 11:00 a.m. on this grief day? I

had counseling. And my counselor helped me with grounding exercises to bring me back into my window of tolerance—which is just a fancy phrase for bringing me back into an emotionally stable place.

And then guess what happened at 3:00 p.m.? I hopped on the phone with a close friend who had gone through betrayal in her marriage as well, just five months after I had, and we talked and cried together. By 4:00 p.m. I had hope pumping through my veins again. Because sometimes it isn't the painful thing that crushes us; it's going through it alone that does.

After being in counseling for the past nine years and attending multiple healing retreats, intensives, and courses on healing, I've realized two things.

1. We never stop healing.

We live in a dark and fallen world under a curse, which wasn't God's original design. When He created Adam and Eve, He created them to be "fruitful and increase in number; fill the earth and subdue it. Rule over the fish in the sea and the birds in the sky and over every living creature that moves on the ground" (Genesis 1:28). He created them with the intention to be blessed and to have humble power over everything. We were designed for a beautiful coleadership position with the Creator of the universe. And then evil stepped into our connected union with God, and pain, sorrow, suffering, and deep grief entered our stories.

The painful stuff is coming. I don't say that to scare you. I actually hope it gives you peace, like it does me. Because it means I'm not crazy for thinking the bad stuff is coming—it actually is. And you're not crazy for thinking about how dark our world is—it is. The pain you've gone through is real. Can we just sit in that for a moment? Can we grieve that there is an enemy of our souls—the serpent in the book of Genesis that tempted Eve in the garden to eat the fruit of a tree that God had said not to eat and ultimately stole our perfect, connected union with our Creator (Genesis 3:1–7)?

I mean, I don't know about you, but I really do wish we could have a do-over. I want to frolic in the grass in complete freedom, without a care in the world! I don't want to worry about my children. I know you don't either. Who wants to worry about finances and sickness and toxic relationships and church hurt? We're not crazy to think that this world is ghetto and jacked up, because—*surprise*—it actually is!

And we don't have to hold that grief alone.

2. Healing doesn't happen alone.

I have a strong belief that there is only one way for us to manage the pain that the darkness in the world causes—together. Lean in right here. The anxiety and depression and sleepless nights could be waiting on a trusted, licensed Christian counselor to teach you grounding exercises. And yes, maybe the way your marriage ended feels like it'll crush you. I know that pain. And the only thing that got me through the grief that felt like a tearing and ripping was a group of my closest people, who offered Band-Aids that held me together until I had the capacity for the emotional surgery I really needed.

Maybe you have friends and you've kept them at the surface for far too long. Maybe you've been deeply hurt by your community, which prevents you from wanting to trust anyone again. I know it's hard. I don't blame you. *When we love hard, we get hurt hard too.* And (not *but*) we don't have another choice. We were designed for community and withness. We won't survive this life without it.

Healing Happens in Community

I received a text from my friend Belinda today. She's walked with me through this past season of devastation and divorce.

> You're inspiring me to work on my recovery time when I feel overwhelmed, frustrated, and out of control. Also, on how to alter my perspective so I can better view how God is working on my behalf, even when I get in my own way. Thank you for that. I know you're impacting and changing lives because you're doing it with me just by being yourself. What a blessing!

That's the impact of healing in community. Not only does it change you, but it heals the people who get to walk with you. They get a front-row seat to what God is doing in your life, and maybe it grows their hope that He'll do it for them too. Maybe it'll remind them that they don't have to heal alone either. What a gift.

That's what I deeply want this book to be for you. A reminder, a tool that will fight the belief that healing is best done alone. Healing alone actually makes it harder. I want you to read this book and allow it to create a reflex in you when you're in pain. A reflex that says, "I need God right now, and I need His people too."

- Tragedy hits your family. God and His people.
- A failed test. Beeline to God and His people.
- The decision to leave a marriage that is no longer God-honoring. God and His people.
- The devastating news that the doctors can't find the heartbeat. God and His people.
- The terrible diagnosis. Let God and His people cover you.
- The moment they found out your sin. Let God and His people lead you to conviction.
- That job let you go. Let God and His people provide for you.

This is the way forward. There's no other way. Our bodies are wired for togetherness. And when we fight our God-given wiring for connection, we not only end up attempting hard things alone but we risk not being able to succeed in them at all.

There are a few things that make us think that we can or should heal alone. And we have to address those lies before we can fully embrace healing in community. Let's dive in and shed the light of some truth on those lies.

Think on This

- Is there a time when you felt alone? Can you imagine Jesus sitting in that place with you and gently saying, "Daughter, there's a difference between being alone and feeling lonely. I am with you so you're never alone. And it's okay to feel lonely."
- Now close your eyes and imagine the God of the universe, the God who is with you, sitting next to you. He's right there.

Part 1

WHY YOU TRY TO HEAL ALONE

Chapter 2

YOU DON'T FEEL SEEN, SOOTHED, SAFE, OR SECURE

I am not naive or ignorant to the fact that you may be reading this and are currently going through something hard, or have gone through something hard, alone. Maybe you've been deeply betrayed by your community. I want to pause and validate that and let you know that, in a few chapters, we'll address that more deeply. For now I want to paint a picture for you. *Let's get our hands dirty.*

I created and get to lead a healing community group twice a year called 100 Hopeful Women. It's a group of women all fighting for hope in the midst of really difficult moments.[1] Typically, the women who sign up are experiencing the worst kind of pain—pain lived alone. And on our first call—which usually lasts around three hours—these beautiful women share the most painful parts of what they're walking through.

Women like Njeri, who lives in South Africa and shared that her husband is a serial cheater and has given her AIDS, but she isn't able to leave him because she doesn't have enough income and feels incredibly alone. So she logs on to our Zoom calls to be seen and reminded that she's not alone on her journey to freedom from deep betrayal.

Women like Cheyenne, who feels her siblings and friends have gone off and met the loves of their lives while she's in a season of longing that will never let up. So she's determined to be a part of something that helps her feel soothed when there's no one around to rub her back. She hops on our Zoom calls with her fur baby—it's my favorite.

There are others in our healing community, like Susan, who lives with a disability and, because of the multiple procedures she's had, has gained unwanted weight and can't seem to please her mother. *You read that right.* Her mother, the person who's supposed to provide the most comfort, is her biggest critic. And she's with us now because she has a longing to feel safe in her body without outside judgment.

And then there's Rochelle, who wants nothing more than to have a healthy marriage. But she's separated and longing for her husband, who has not been communicating his reasoning for leaving, to come home. She feels wobbly, confused, and anxious. She doesn't know what to expect or how to plan or if he'll ever come back. She longs for surety and to feel secure.

And then there's you. The one who God knows everything about. He knows every tear you've cried and how you grabbed this book longing to be seen, soothed, safe, and secure. To not be alone in the pain. To get good at finding good people. To not make the same mistakes. To experience the real power of withness. To be more whole and more healed and less alone.

The Power of Doing Life Together

Whether we like it or not, when we are alone—whether we decided to isolate or we've been abandoned and refuse to try again—we miss the opportunity to fulfill our core longings and have healthy attachments with people. We end up living in the reality of our greatest fear—being alone. And alongside those longings is the fact that God wired us to have them be fulfilled through togetherness.

When we look at the life of Jesus as He walked the earth, we can see that from His first breath He quite literally knew the power of doing life with people in the midst of hard things. (Go with me here; it's time to use our imagination like we used to when we were little girls.) God, the Creator of the whole entire everything, could've decided to just plop Jesus right onto earth, but His plan included Jesus being born into a family. Mary and Joseph together facing the shame that Mary was pregnant in the first place. Together facing rejection and being turned away to deliver the Savior of the universe into this world. Together in the hard and together in the laboring and the birthing of Jesus. He entered this world teaching us that family matters—that togetherness matters.

One of my good friends, Charlene, lives in a shelter here in Atlanta where I get to serve. (I'm changing her name to protect her safety here, but her story won't be less powerful because of it.) I usually volunteer on Monday mornings at 10:00, and as I walked into my first group session with the ladies who live there, I couldn't help but notice Charlene sitting sideways at one of the tables, with her feet kicked up on another chair.

I just thought, *Well, I guess a girl's gotta get comfortable up in here.* I introduced myself to the room, told them what I did, why I was there, and how excited I was to see what God was going to do through our time together over the months or even years. I shared some hard parts of my story, both as a bid for shame to leave the room and to start honest connection with the women. And then I asked them to be a little brave and tell me their names and something they wanted me to know about them. One by one they shared, and I beamed with joy that I was in this room with kindred spirits.

Then it was Charlene's turn. "Hey, y'all. My name is Charlene. I'm a survivor of abuse and trafficking, and I've been sober for a few months now. Oh—and I'm pregnant with a little girl."

Oh. *That's* why she was sitting that way. Her belly couldn't fit under the table if she faced forward, so she'd turned to the side.

After introductions I taught a little on John 8:1–11 and how the woman who'd been caught in the act of adultery probably had so much shame walking into the temple courts and what she thought would be her death. Instead, she walked into her freedom. Jesus ended up showing her grace and calling her into a life turning away from sin. He didn't condemn her.

Every woman in the room could relate to this story. Every woman in the room wanted this type of freedom and deep connection with Jesus. And then I told them something that I don't think many of them had heard before: "You can most definitely experience this type of connection with Jesus, *and* you can also experience it with us right now."

"Whatcha mean?" Charlene blurted out. "Everyone I've ever trusted has abandoned me, hurt me, or lied to me. I'm gonna be alone having my little girl. I don't got nobody."

Then something holy happened. Lily, an older Black woman in the shelter, said, "You a lie! You gone have to claw me out of the delivery room! They gone have to kick me out, honey, because I'm gone be right there cuddling that sweet baby girl!"

Charlene's eyes filled with tears. The room got silent. Then I think all of us felt it—withness. The power of people coming for you and not ever leaving the room. But for many of us, like Charlene, we don't know what that feels like. It's foreign and weird, and it doesn't dawn on us that it even exists. Charlene reminded us of what it's like to be unseen, unsoothed, unsafe, and unsecure. And honestly, if we are going to fight for withness, we might first need to just sit in what it feels like to be alone.

You're not alone in your longings to be seen, soothed, safe, and secure. Those longings start at a really early age, and if they aren't met, it affects the way we form attachments with people throughout our lives.

You're not alone in your longings to be seen, soothed, safe, and secure.

The 4 S's

My dear friend and a Christian psychiatrist, Dr. Curt Thompson, described this longing for attachment this way: "We all come into this world looking for someone looking for us."[2]

In *The Power of Showing Up*, authors Dan Siegel and Tina Bryson elaborate on and describe a secure attachment as being made up of four things. In their words,

> When children feel safe, seen (being known and understood), and soothed (being helped to feel calm and good again) most of the time (not perfectly), they develop security (where their brain wires to expect that people will see their needs and show up for them). This is applicable in all of our relationships—when we don't know what to do or how to respond, we can turn to the 4 S's to instruct us—we show up, and when we are having a hard time, we can seek out people who will help us feel the 4 S's.[3]

Let's think about that for a second. Basically we all need to feel seen, soothed, safe, and secure. But what if we don't feel one or two or all of those things?

1. You don't feel seen.

When you're unseen, you question everything about yourself and the way that God made you. If God really made you this way, why are you so hard to love and be around? You might also feel like

- nobody knows the real you (and maybe if they did, they wouldn't stay around),
- people don't understand you (or even try to), and
- you've been hiding for so long that you don't know how to walk into the light—it's too scary and foreign.

God designed you on purpose and with incredible intention. It's not that who He made you to be is hard to be around; it's possible that you have the wrong people around in the first place. You, Charlene, Lily, Jamie, Jess, and I are made in His divine and creative image. Seeing you—deeply seeing and knowing you—is a privilege.

2. You don't feel soothed.

If you're not soothed when you're hurting, it feels like the worst kind of emotional betrayal. One of the moments I think about when it comes to being unsoothed was in middle school. I wanted to do something different with my hair for picture day, and my mom was too sick at the time to help. A few days before picture day, I glued in pieces of fake hair to my scalp, and it looked terrible. You know that little doll from the *Rugrats* named Cynthia? That's the kind of vibe my hair was going through. (If you don't know who Cynthia is, please google "Rugrats doll Cynthia" and get a good laugh.)

I tried to rip out the fake hair the morning of picture day and ended up losing a lot of my real hair. I was so embarrassed; I didn't want to have to dress myself and do my own hair for picture day—I wanted my mom to, but she just couldn't. I looked terrible and had no one to wipe my tears as I sat in the girls' bathroom at Wunderlich Intermediate School in Houston, Texas, longing for someone to hold me and tell me it was going to be okay.

When we are left alone in our pain with no one to wipe our tears, that's the feeling of being unsoothed. It can also feel like

- your feelings have been dismissed and labeled as "too much" or you were told that you're "too sensitive,"
- in the face of your greatest pain, you had to be strong and tough it out,
- you can't think of one person you could call and just cry on the phone with, and
- you're the strong friend who shows up for everyone, but no one shows up for you.

Lean into this idea: No matter how strong you've had to be, and what you had to do to survive, you deserve to be soothed. You were designed to be soothed when the pain feels like it'll crush you. And longing for that soothing is not at all an act of weakness—it's a fulfillment of the bravery of longing for the comfort that our bodies need.

3. You don't feel safe.

If you've ever felt unsafe in your healing journey, I'm so sorry. I hate when people gossip and share things that someone has told them in private. It just sucks, and it breaches safety in us to the point where it's hard to trust again. A few things can lead to feeling unsafe as you heal.

- You voice your feelings and they're somehow turned back on you.
- You talk about your pain and it's used against you.
- You've voiced things in secrecy only to have them shared as gossip.
- You've been told your emotions are excuses.
- You sought out a "safe space" only for it to hurt you in the end.

Gossip isn't a pathway to connection; it leads only to disruption. Disruption of the way that God designed us to heal together in the presence of His safe people. The bad experiences you've had when someone breached your trust don't get to derail your healing. Getting up, trusting again, believing in God's people again, and trying to press into vulnerability will always be worth it. No one gets to take that away from you, okay?

4. You don't feel secure.

Finally, not feeling secure is really about not having healthy attachments to people, which is a direct result of us not having the other three needs (safety, soothing, and being seen) met. This makes it difficult to have healthy, secure relationships, and it feels like

- you don't have any meaningful relationships that can hold your pain,
- you have unhealthy or toxic relationships,
- you have difficulty naming your own emotions because doing so was never modeled for you, and

- you're unable to regulate your emotions and you have no one to help.

We need to feel seen, soothed, and safe so we can form secure attachments. These 4 S's are like our emotional fuel to healthy connection. They affect not only our romantic relationships but our connection to our parents, our friends, our children, and even the people we get to work with. This is worth fighting for, friend. And it will for sure be a fight.

If any of these points resonated with you in any way, I just want to stop again and say I'm sorry. I see you, and I have felt every single one of the experiences on that list. But we can't let them keep us in isolation. Evil actually wants you to heal alone because that's when you're the weakest. I don't have to tell you this—you know.

You know that temptation is easier to fall into when there's no accountability. You know that it's easier to numb with wine, alcohol, shopping, overdoing it in the gym, and yelling and screaming than it is to just say the thing to someone close so that you can start the healing process. Satan wants us in isolation so that we can fail alone and not have someone to rescue us because no one even knows we've fallen.

Let's Not Repeat the Garden

Now, there's some theological argument to this, but my theory about Genesis 3—when the serpent and Eve were having a conversation about her eating the forbidden fruit that God told her not to eat—is that maybe initially Adam wasn't present and that's how the serpent got Eve to fold.

> Now the serpent was more crafty than any of the wild animals the LORD God had made. He said to the woman, "Did God really say, 'You must not eat from any tree in the garden'?"
>
> The woman said to the serpent, "We may eat fruit from the trees in the garden, but God did say, 'You must not eat fruit from the tree that is in the middle of the garden, and you must not touch it, or you will die.'"
>
> "You will not certainly die," the serpent said to the woman. "For God knows that when you eat from it your eyes will be opened, and you will be like God, knowing good and evil." (vv. 1–5)

While Adam eventually ate the fruit as well, the Bible never says the serpent spoke to Adam, only Eve. I find it very peculiar that Adam would just stand there and not say anything—especially regarding a decision that God was so vehemently against. Eve didn't have her covering, and it cost them both connection with God.

But it ultimately didn't cost us. Instead, we are now living in the reconnection era of Christ. Jesus came to give us back one of the most important things we have—connection. First with our heavenly Father, then with His people. Jesus died for this connection because of how important it is. We weren't created to live alone, and we don't have to live, breathe, work out, work, worship, or heal alone. It's always better together.

At this point you're probably thinking, *Okay, Toni, how do I do this well? How do I move from isolation and hiding into togetherness with people, even when I don't feel like it? How do I learn to trust again? How do I push past the hurt and lean into connection?*

In the next chapter we get to talk about my favorite *S*-word—shame. It's become a favorite not because it's fun but because I've figured out how to drain its power! If there was a scheme of the enemy outside of getting Eve to eat that darn fruit, it would be shame. We need to dive into it, dissect it, identify it, heal from it, and kick it to the curb. On the other side of shame, I think, is a freedom that's needed for deep connection. Let's go!

Think on This

- Out of the 4 S's, which one is the most absent from your life?

    1. You don't feel seen.
    2. You don't feel soothed.
    3. You don't feel safe.
    4. You don't feel secure.

- Is there a moment when you can recall feeling unseen, unsoothed, unsafe, or unsecure? How does that moment affect you today? Think about some of the feelings that moment brings up and how it's keeping you from connecting deeply with your community.

Chapter 3

YOUR SHAME KEEPS YOU ISOLATED

Never in a million years did I think I'd be on a nine-month, multicity salvation tour. This thought crossed my mind as I sat in the front row of a church in Allentown, Pennsylvania. I'd been asked by my good friend Karrie to go on the road with her and her team for the seventh year of their tour to churches around America. This tour was different—it wasn't just about singing songs with fellow Christians to further solidify our relationship and intimacy with God. It was about bringing people to Christ who had never said yes to Him. It was about our greatest mission: to spread the gospel to the ends of the earth (Mark 16:15).

This was the trenches—my kind of place. We went to city after city and witnessed women being set free, stepping into the light that is the truth of who Jesus is and who He created them to be. Listen, it was beautiful. To see people who were in their thirties, sixties, and even seventies say yes to Jesus at the end of the night for the first time was the most rewarding thing I'd ever done. It was the gospel. And if anyone asked me what I thought the secret sauce was, I'd say it was Karrie's story.

Karrie is the founder of Freedom Movement—the organization that invited me to go on tour. She's a good friend, partially because we both have the wildest, funniest stories and are crazy about Jesus. I remember sitting on the front row of that church in Pennsylvania as she told her story. She was in a marriage that ended because of her. She was the betrayer. I could feel the air leave the room when she confessed that to hundreds of strangers. Karrie also explained that she lost her mother to suicide because of the pressures of church culture that her mom was thrust into without space to hold her mental illness. During this time Karrie was on crystal meth, which is a drug that is highly addictive and super dangerous to your body and mind. And in the middle of all this, there was a moment behind the wheel of a car—broken, lost, alone, and parked at a red light—when she decided she didn't want to live anymore.

Writing that makes me teary right now just like when I was in the room in Pennsylvania. I love Karrie, and knowing what the other side of this story looked like gave me so much hope for the other women in the room. I knew her story, so I knew that the light was coming to her darkness—and I couldn't wait for the women to know it as well.

Karrie had been planning to drive into oncoming traffic. The weight of life was really hard, but even harder was the shame. She couldn't hold the shame: The reality that she had ruined her marriage. The sorrow and regret from being unable to save her mom from the very thing that Karrie was now facing. I imagine she asked some questions that maybe you've asked before:

- How did I get here?
- How can I go on?
- Where is God?
- Will anyone love me?
- Is anyone coming for me?
- Will anyone miss me?
- Is my family embarrassed by me?
- Am I so weak that I can't handle this?

And then God did what God does—He spoke to her. For the first time in her life Karrie heard the voice of God. "Stay" was all He said. She wept. And then she stayed. And she lived to tell the story in a room of women longing to stay and not knowing how. Shame didn't win.

What Shame Is

"Shame" is such a hot word now. Hotter than a fresh Krispy Kreme doughnut when the red Hot light clicks on. (Google it, trust me.) Everyone's using this word, and typically when things are used a lot, they get watered down or feel lame to talk about. But lean in right here as I say this: *If there was a scheme of the enemy, it would be shame.* This is absolutely the devil's playing field when it comes to separating us from people when we are hurting. Because if he can make us feel shame he can make us hide, and if he can make us hide we won't get any help, and if we don't have help we don't have healing. Shame is his best work. Which is kind of a weird thing to say about the enemy of our souls. But he's intelligent evil, girl. He's not an outsider to what God wants to do in our lives. He's a fallen angel who believes and knows the power of our God. His goal is different, however; it's to steal, kill, and destroy God's creation—you (John 10:10).

I want to take a second to get nerdy with my friend Dr. Curt Thompson. Here's how he describes shame in an interview with the Council for Christian Colleges and Universities *Advance* magazine:

> If you look at the [psychology] literature, shame is understood as an artifact of nature—it just happens to be something that we experience. We don't like it, but there's not much we can do about it other than regulate it. But if you read the biblical narrative, it would suggest that shame's actually not just an artifact—it's a vector. It's something that evil is actively and intentionally using to disintegrate the universe and to devour it. There is an intention behind it.[1]

Curt's statement on shame is so freeing. If we can each realize that shame isn't a past thing but a living thing that invades all our thoughts and feelings—starting with feelings of embarrassment when we were around three or four years old—we can break free. We all deal with shame. Let me pause and repeat that so you can feel it. Your neighbor, your mama, your cousins, your crush, your trainer, your pastor—*all of them deal with shame.* So here's a good and possibly freeing reminder for us all: We can't get rid of shame, but we can manage it in healthy ways.

How to Manage Shame

I'm hoping that when you're done reading this chapter, you'll believe that you actually can manage shame. It won't be easy, because shame is also really sneaky, but here are a few things that have helped me.

1. Stop hiding.

When our favorite pastor, worship leader, or Bible teacher loses their church or platform due to a moral failure, everyone's shocked. Why? Well, because no one saw it coming! The leader was hiding! Shame makes us hide. Shame is an identity attacker. It forces us into a dark place with voices that spew lies like "I am unworthy of good things. My past does discount me. I should hide because I'm too broken to be used anyway." If hiding is the kryptonite to healing, shame is the villain in the story, ready to defeat us by taking away the very things God designed us for—connection and witness.

Defeating shame will cost you. I'm not trying to scare you from facing it, but I'm a no-fluff kind of girl. At this point in my life, with all the trauma in my story, I'm out to set some people free, so I'm gonna say the thing! It's going to cost you to stop hiding. It's going to push you past your instinct to hide, and I don't want to pretend that it's not hard to step into the light. It's terrible and sometimes embarrassing and absolutely worth it. It will always be worth it to get out of hiding. Let me show you why.

If the shame in you says, *I don't want anyone to know*, not only will you have to walk through the reality of the pain you're healing from but you'll also be doing it alone. When the anxiety hits, you won't have someone reminding you to breathe when it feels like the grief is suffocating you. When depression hits, you won't have anyone to encourage you that maybe the best you can do today is take a shower and celebrate that. When you're feeling unwanted because your single season is taking far too long for your heart, you won't have a gal friend who sends coffee or a mani-pedi on her. You'll also risk someone finding out instead of you willingly telling them. And when someone finds out you're going through something hard alone, the connection you really want is thrust onto you versus being gently invited in. Connection by invitation is always sweeter than by discovery.

I'm a mom to two cutie babies, and my oldest, Dylan, has officially stepped into her tween years. When she gets in the car after school with a sad face or her eyes rolling to the back of her head, my first question is, "What's going on, babe?" and my second is, "Do you want to talk about it?" Now, I'm gonna be real here: I'm not a chill mom—I want to know all the things immediately. I don't want to ask if she wants to talk about it,

It will always be worth it to get out of hiding.

because I am ready to talk about it *now*. I want to get to the bottom of it and find solutions. I want her to be all better.

Initially she often says that she doesn't want to talk about it. And I've got to tell you, those are my worst parenting moments because I can't get it off my mind. Ten minutes into the drive home, I'm already asking if she's sure she doesn't want to talk about it. And she typically says no, and the truth is we lose out on connection, and she has to sit alone with whatever has bothered her at school alone. And then, when she's ready—and not before—she comes into my bedroom after I've put my little son, Sammie, to bed at 7:00 p.m. and we've done our face masks. She plops on my bed and tells everything. She talks about the boy in school who pushed her and when she pushed him back, she was the one who got in trouble. She talks about how life isn't fair, and school sucks sometimes. She talks about how she was embarrassed that she let her anger get the best of her and made bad choices because of it. She invites me into her feelings.

Here is the inception point of our connection. Here's my opportunity to let Dylan know that she's not alone, school does suck sometimes, and she can be brave enough to apologize even when it doesn't feel fair. This is my opportunity to let Dylan know that shame doesn't have to win, and when she invites me in, I can help her defeat it. This is what her good body that God made longs for—not to escape the inescapable (shame) but to really be seen, even in her mistakes and shame. The truth is Dylan needed me to come for her and remind her that who she is will always matter more than what she has done wrong.

2. Have faith that you will not be abandoned by God or your people.

Okay, here's another thing that the shame in you can say: *They'd leave me if they knew the truth. They'll look at me differently.* Let's get real honest here. Whether you've been the victim of something terrible or you've caused pain to others, once you share your story openly with your people, they may leave you or view you differently. In fact, you may be reading this with a person in mind who's done these very things to you. I'm sorry that in the midst of your shame and pain you were left to think you were anything less than lovable. We are broken and flawed human beings, and I just don't want to promise perfection from an imperfect world.

Let me give you some hope, though. The fingerprint of deep, trusted community is that your people will not leave you in pain, and they will always look at you as a child of God. This is why it's extremely important to practice finding and leaning into community over time. To build trust and deep connection so that when hard times come, there's something in your community's "reserve" to withstand the reality of holding brokenness together.

While writing this book, a close friend in our confessional community and I both experienced spousal betrayal. It rocked our group. We didn't ever think that I would be staring at divorce for the second time or that our dear friend would be wading through the trauma of public betrayal—in detail—over and over again.

This is when we lean in and remind each other that no matter what we've been through or what's tried to take us out—or even what pain or mistakes we've made along the way while doing our best to heal—safe, healthy community always does two things well. First, they don't leave you, especially when you're down. Second, they always, always look at you through the lens of what God sees: forgiven, worthy of redemption, fearlessly loved, and an heir to His throne. This is who you are in the eyes of God and who you should be in the eyes of His people.

3. Trust that you will find safe people.

The last thing that shame may say targets your community: "They're unsafe. They'll tell other people." This is another really hard one, because the truth is that the reason you even have this belief is probably because you've experienced unsafe people. In Lysa TerKeurst's book *Forgiving What You Can't Forget*, she says, "Staying here, blaming them, and forever defining your life by what they did will only increase the pain. Worse, it will keep projecting out onto others. The more our pain consumes us, the more it will control us. And sadly, it's those who least deserve to be hurt whom our unresolved pain will hurt the most."[2] Staying in the pain of what others have done to you will keep you stuck and isolated. Not only that but the bitterness and isolation that come with keeping people at bay while you try to heal alone will also take away your opportunity to *be* healthy community for others.

Getting up again and trying to heal with others is the only way. Trusting again is the only way. And I'm not saying your hesitancy to trust is unwarranted. The pain that I have experienced at the hands of other people, especially publicly, is one of the most disappointing parts of my story. But I will not dare allow the actions of imperfect humans to steal the gift of connection and withness that our perfect God has designed. They may have caused my tears and even my heartbreak, but they don't get to have this. They don't get to have my connection with people.

God's Design

We cannot shrink back from God's design. He designed us for community, for deep confession and communion with one another. We are a connected creation. It's no surprise that the enemy of our souls wants this part of our story. But he doesn't get to have it. Nope, nope, nope.

Death to shame!

Wow, that was a little aggressive, but I got riled up! Shame is a scheme of the enemy, but it won't work against people who refuse to hide, who know they will not be abandoned by their God or their people, and who believe they will find safe community—people like you, who are reading this book and making the conscious decision to lean into the healing journey hand in hand instead of hiding. So let's end with some agreements and declarations around shame. If you need to return to them a few times or even every day until you believe them, fold this page's corner into a nice little mini taco, or tap the bookmark on your screen, and keep coming back here to get these truths into you:

- I won't allow shame to cause me to hide things that I've done, because it will hinder my freedom and healing.
- I won't allow shame to put fear in me that people will always leave me. I will decide to heal again and trust again.
- I won't allow shame to take away my identity. I am forgiven, worthy of redemption, fearlessly loved, and an heir to the throne of God.
- I won't allow shame to make me believe that everyone is untrustworthy. I will rebuild my trust in humanity and invite safe people in so that I can get the healing I need.

Think on This

- Which one of the three ways to manage shame is the hardest for you?
- Which of the three ways to manage shame is the most effective for you?
- Can you think of a time when shame made it difficult for you to trust again?

I want to encourage you to write two or three sentences that you will speak over yourself when shame shows up. If you're struggling to come up with your own, use mine: *Shame doesn't get the final say in my life. It might show up, it might put up a good fight, but it can't have my freedom to be exactly who God made me to be.*

Now let's take a deep breath in, hold it for four seconds, and exhale for six seconds. One more time. Inhale, hold it, exhale. See you in chapter 4. You're doing great.

Chapter 4

YOU'RE AFRAID OF BEING FOUND

I remember the moment my son, Sammie, learned how to play peekaboo. It was precious. I had set him down on his changing table and was trying to peel his little pajama top over his head. It was a tight squeeze, let me just say that. Wooh, that head! I could tell he was getting irritated by how slowly the too-tight dinosaur top was coming off, so I started playing peekaboo with it to distract him. He loved it. He giggled and showed off his two little pearly whites and pink gums as I went back and forth between squeezing the shirt off and surprising him with a peekaboo in between.

It became his favorite game. Soon it morphed into hide-and-seek. I can still hear him and his "sissy," my daughter, Dylan, running around the house playing together. One time I was sitting on our living room couch watching them play hide-and-seek. Sammie could barely get any words out between the cackles he belted out every time Dylan found him. He was only two years old, so those hiding spots were easy to find. Sammie would hide next to the couch, not behind it, and Dylan would pretend she didn't see him for a while, calling out, "Where's Sammie?" until she crept around the corner and yelled, "I got you!" And there went those little cackles again. I think I loved the innocence of him believing he was hiding but being seen all along.

I wonder how many times we've found ourselves believing that we're doing a great job at hiding, when all along everything can be seen. We've tried to get good at hiding our pain, but God sees. Our close people—they see. When we were younger, our parents saw. In my first book on healing, *Brave Enough to Be Broken*, one of the quotes that people loved to reference in interviews or podcasts was "Hiding is the kryptonite to healing." It really is. In order to start healing, we have to stop hiding. It's not working anyway. Whether we like it or not, our stuff always eventually surfaces.

I used to sneak out of the house in high school to meet up with a guy. I thought I was doing a real good job of hiding it too. I used to put pillows and stuffed animals under my blanket, slip out of my room, walk across the hall to what used to be my brother's room, move the dresser that was in front of the window, and climb out to skip around town and be completely unruly with a guy who was okay with enabling my hiding—instead of encouraging me to just tell my parents about him. It was all smooth sailing until one day, as I was climbing back through the window after one of my escapades with him, I saw the silhouette of my mom in the doorframe. I froze mid-climb. *She'd gotten me.* The hiding was over. She wanted—*demanded*—answers. Rightfully so. What began as a masterful plan I'd carried out for months had now been forced into the light. Here's the truth: Walking into the light is a heck of a lot better than being forced into the light.

Maybe you're battling an eating disorder. It's only so long before someone is going to realize that you disappear every time you eat, and you come back to the table pale and disheveled.

Maybe you're watching inappropriate things to numb the pain of not being touched and feeling forever lonely. It's only a matter of time before conviction settles in or someone accidentally sees your search history.

Cutting corners at work because you're feeling overwhelmed by the weight of everything? Your boss finding out and you losing your job could be just around the corner.

Cheating on your spouse who once betrayed you to fill the trust gap you can't seem to escape? Hurting those who hurt you is a game that always ends with multiple losers.

Gossiping about your friend to avoid conflict because you haven't found healthy ways to express your pain? She will find out, and that will make it worse. Ever text the wrong person something you didn't want them to see—something about them?

Hiding never works.

Hiding makes things worse.

Hiding is the kryptonite to healing, and being found out is

not a punishment; it's an invitation to a better way of healing. God reveals only to heal. He wants your pain to come into the light so that it can be divinely touched by Him and tenderly held by His people. Revealing your pain is not a punishment, it's care. It's the God of the universe coming to find you because hiding is lonely. The whole goal of hide-and-seek is to keep anyone from finding you, and that's just not a game we can play with our hurting hearts. We need to be found; we need to be seen.

How to Stop Hiding

I think about how Psalm 34:18 promises that "the LORD is close to the brokenhearted and saves those who are crushed in spirit." I don't know about you, but I want closeness when I am hurting. The problem is there's something that threatens that closeness: avoidance. Avoiding the awkwardness of telling someone you're hurting or embarrassed or feeling betrayed is a sure way to not heal from your hurt, embarrassment, and betrayal. So how do we do this well? Let's get practical!

1. Surround yourself with people who won't let you hide.

This is a hard one because the easy choice is to have friends who won't come after you. Friends who may see you're in pain but aren't emotionally savvy enough to do something about it. I remember when I first met friends who came after me. They would call on days I didn't feel like talking. Ask questions that I didn't want to answer and challenge me to talk about my pain anyway. It was annoying at first, if I'm honest. I was so used to stuffing my pain and just "dealing with it" the way I was taught growing up. Emotions were excuses to my nine-year-old heart. And excuses make you weak. But then I realized that true bravery costs you something. It costs you picking up the phone when you don't feel like it. It costs you talking about the thing that you didn't want to have to explain and relive, pressing in when the only thing you want to do is tap out. That's real bravery and strength—not weakness. It's far from weakness.

Get around people who won't let you hide. Talk openly. Tell them that is what you want, even when you don't want it. And tell them when you're not in pain or crisis. Be on the offense, not the defense, when it comes to your healing. Text or say something like, "Hey, I usually make a beeline to hiding when I am hurting or in pain. Can you make sure I don't hide? Can you call me even when you think it'll annoy me? Can you come for me?" That being said, when you're in crisis mode and can feel yourself wanting to hide, that, too, may be the moment to text a friend.

I found myself wanting to hide on my first Father's Day as a single mom. I wanted to curl up in a ball in my bed and never leave my house again. I told three friends via text, "I'm taking a nap, but I really don't ever want to get up and face life again. I'm just telling you for accountability." This was my white flag, my SOS. It is how I refused to hide.

2. Choose to be accountable to someone.

It's not enough to not hide; it also matters what we're doing when we hide. For me, it's alcohol. When I am in pain, I want to numb that pain so that I can show up and perform. That's my default, and it's not the healthy option. Hide it, numb it, and it will crush you. Honestly, I've seen what it looks like to choose this option one too many times in my life. But no more. As soon as I feel the urge to drink in an attempt to numb my pain, I phone a friend. Debra has been that friend in this season. She's been the one who is direct and honest with me, who pulls no punches, and who points me to Jesus. She's incredible. You need a Debra in your life.

Another reason we have to choose accountability is that we naturally drift toward chaos. Accountability is an act of radical humility. Humility says, "I am broken and imperfect and living under the curse of sin." Humility recognizes that we are flawed even when we're not in pain. So just imagine what we're susceptible to when we're in real pain!

Get your accountability in place before you face the pains that naturally come with life. Prepare yourself for chaos so that you can live in peace and protection when it comes. But it will require humility and acceptance of your imperfections. And it'll be the best choice you can make right now for later on.

3. Look for the light.

Look for the good and the hope that is undoubtedly around you. While we need to expect pain in our lives, we should also know that we don't have to stay in the valleys. A beautiful way to stop hiding is to switch your perspective from "Darkness is here, and it will consume me" to "There's always light to be found. Where is it?" Where is the light? Is it a mani-pedi day with your friends? Is it a massage? Is it playing at the park with your children? Is it found in your journal where you can process your emotions? Is it in a cozy bubble bath? What brings you back to mountains of hope after valleys of despair? What gets you out of bed after days of staying in it without a shower in sight? So many of us are still stuck in darkness. Whether we don't know that there's light to be found, or we're too weary to look for it, or we've hit a point of hopelessness, we don't have to stay stuck. Sometimes all we need is a friend to use their free ticket to invite us to a conference with some crazy women who love Jesus but are honest enough to tell the hard parts of their stories to remind us that hope is on the way. Friend, it's coming. The light is coming for you. Make sure you're keeping watch.

4. Expect to be found.

Sometimes the problem isn't that we don't want to be found, it's that we don't think we're worthy enough to be found. Thoughts like *Who really cares about me? Is anyone coming?* are so real. This may be your reality right now. Maybe you haven't been able to build a community, and you don't have anyone reaching out to you when you want to hide from your pain. This isn't easy for everyone. I want to encourage you to start with your own heart. Start with your own beliefs about yourself. Do you believe right now that you're worthy to be found? To be pursued? To be loved and seen—and not just in a romantic way? Do you think you're a burden?

Maybe someone told you that when you were just a little girl. Maybe you were the oldest and you had to carry everyone else's burdens, and no one carried yours. Maybe you've felt like this your whole life, or maybe you just started. Listen to me, please. You were made worthy to be found. From the moment you cried and air filled your lungs, you were made worthy to be deeply seen and pursued. Your heavenly Father designed and created you to be chosen and taken in. If you don't have people who can affirm that for you, it's time for you to claim it over yourself.

Can we practice? Can you repeat this out loud if you're able? "I am worthy to be found. I am worthy to be found. I am worthy to be found."

Can we also say this? "I was created to be chosen. I was created to be chosen. I was created to be chosen." That's right, you were. Without a doubt. Believe that over yourself today.

I think I can remember the very first time I actually wanted to be found. My mom and I were shopping in Walmart, and I decided it would be funny to play a game of hide-and-seek with her, unbeknownst to her. As she was shopping in the clothes section, I slowly crept into one of the circular clothing racks. I sat cross-legged right in the middle, so proud of myself and wondering when my mom would come find me. It grew really quiet, and I got a little nervous, but I couldn't blow my cover.

A few seconds passed that felt like hours. Butterflies were forming in my stomach. Finally I just couldn't take it anymore. My seven-year-old heart was afraid, and I wanted to be found. I popped out of the clothing rack, but I didn't see my mom. I started frantically looking for her, calling, "Mom! Mom! Where are you?"

As the tears welled up in my eyes, I realized I was alone and lost. I didn't know where my mom was. I really wanted to be found. And then I heard her yelling, "Nae! Nae! Where are you? It's Mom. Nae! Where are you?" I could hear the despair and worry in her voice.

I desperately wanted to be found. She desperately wanted to find me. I didn't want to hide anymore. The only place I wanted to hide was in her arms. And then I saw her. I ran up to her, tripping over my feet on the way. "Mom!" I screamed. She was so afraid that she had lost me. I was so afraid that I had lost her.

The best feeling in the world was going from wanting to hide to being found.

Even in this past year, when I desperately wanted to hide my pain from the world; when I was so tired of seeing my name in articles and Google searches; when I wanted to take my children to another country and start over; when I didn't want people to see me so fragile and broken and weak, I refused to hide. Because I know that the God of the universe created me to be chosen and found. And He created you that way too.

No More Hiding

Look at what God says about finding His people:

> Listen to me, family of Jacob, everyone that's left of the family of Israel. I've been carrying you on my back from the day you were born, and I'll keep on carrying you when you're old. I'll be there, bearing you when you're old and gray. I've

The best feeling in the world was going from wanting to hide to being found.

done it and will keep on doing it, carrying you on my back, saving you. (Isaiah 46:3–4 MSG)

Oh, this is such a powerful scripture for our weary, hiding hearts. First of all, how many times have you felt like you had to carry it all yourself? I've got good news: He is the God that carries His people! He has been carrying you from before you took one breath, and He will carry you to the day you breathe your last.

Second, that word "bearing" isn't a negative concept. It's the same idea that shows up in Matthew 10:29–31: "Are not two sparrows sold for a penny? Yet not one of them will fall to the ground outside your Father's care. And even the very hairs of your head are all numbered. So don't be afraid; you are worth more than many sparrows." If God would take such tender care to count the hairs of our heads, He will make sure to keep up with us and carry us when we need it.

And lastly, He will save you. I wish I could hold your hand and look you in the eye and tell you every moment He saved me and my children. I hope these words that you're reading are enough to get you to realize that He is saving you too. Every year, every month, every single millisecond, He's saving you, my dear friend. He is incapable of watching us suffer without being sad about it. He moves from sadness to saving. He is our *moshia'*—the Hebrew word for "Savior."[1] Our Deliverer who delivers every single time.

So no more hiding, okay? No more shrinking back from your healing journey and allowing the enemy of your soul to short-circuit the hope that is coming your way. Come on, lean into this. No more hiding. It's time to get brave, it's time to heal out loud. It's time to begin again, look up again, and let the light hit your face as it was destined to.

Let people in, find the people that will come, choose to humbly be held accountable for the mistakes and numbing in your healing journey. Bask in your worthiness, daughter of God, and watch the floodgates of healing open up for you. Let God, your people, and me in this moment be the ones to say, "I've got you!" We are not letting you go. The darkness won't last. The light is on the way. I promise.

Think on This

- What areas of your life are you hiding?
- What's the top reason for your hiding? Is there someone you can express that to?
- Repeat these words seven times: "The darkness won't last. The light is on the way."

Chapter 5

YOU'VE BEEN HURT BY THE RESPONSES OF THOSE CLOSE TO YOU

Have you ever shared something hard with someone you were close to, and they just responded . . . wrong? Like, the very thing you hoped they would say just didn't come out in their response at all?

I have. After my divorce, I decided to be honest and vulnerable about it on Instagram and how difficult it was to be a single mom. And while I received tons of encouraging messages and prayers, there was one response that I'll never forget: "Well if you didn't have a nanny in your house all the time, your husband probably wouldn't have cheated on you. Stop complaining." I know—ouch. It was an insensitive, ignorant, and unhelpful response. And for some reason, out of the hundreds of beautiful messages I received, that one has always stuck with me. Sometimes painful things last longer than helpful things.

Maybe you can relate to having an unmet expectation around a hard conversation. It could look like voicing to your mom how hard parenting a child of yours with a behavioral diagnosis has been, and her response is, "Just have another kid, this one is just spoiled." And you're left feeling like the very person who should understand the parenting journey, the one who raised you, didn't provide the comfort you craved.

It's expressing to a friend how it feels like the grief of losing a child will never let up, and their response is, "Good thing you have another child, so it's okay." And you're left feeling like maybe you're wrong or ungrateful for being sad about losing a child.

It could be telling a small-group leader that you just lost your job and you're having a hard time with finances, and instead of comfort the response is, "But my God shall supply all your needs according to his riches in glory by Christ Jesus" (Philippians 4:19 KJV). And you're left feeling like God is transactional and doesn't care about your feelings.

It's crying to your bestie about a hard breakup you're walking through and she's hollering, "Get over it, girl! He was ugly anyway; you can do better!" And now you feel alone in your grief and maybe pressured to move on to another guy. When really you thought he was the cutest man walking but now you aren't feeling safe enough to admit that.

It's finally getting to a place where you can admit to a close friend that you've struggled with lust and porn, and they begin to distance themselves from you. And now the lie you believe is that when you make a mistake and share it openly, you'll be abandoned.

It's expressing to your counselor a negative sexual experience you had and having him fall asleep mid-session, leaving you feeling more alone in your sexuality than you did before you got there. (Yes, this is a true story; a counselor fell asleep on me once. Yikes!)

I've said this before and I'll say it again: I don't want to pretend that healing in community is a Care Bears parade where everyone is bopping around on clouds singing "Hakuna Matata" all the time. People will say and do the wrong things in response to your pain. People will make it difficult for you to heal together instead of alone. People will throw scriptures at you instead of showing up with curiosity and care. They'll leave because they're uncomfortable. They'll lead with correction before comfort.

The truth is, when we are in pain, we don't want correction; we want comfort. It's messy and beautiful, holy and hard, imperfect and scary—and it'll always be worth it. We were designed for companionship and to carry each other's burdens (Galatians 6:2). We are a connected creation. Our support and prayer for each other have the power to heal us (James 5:16). And, through thick and thin, when we choose to love, we create safety for each other (Proverbs 17:17).

Why People Give Problematic Responses

While all of those encouraging scriptures are true, we will still encounter moments in our relationships when we get hurt while we are trying to heal. What we can do about it now is simply know what to look out for and why it's happening, and manage our response to it in healthy ways. There are a few reasons people respond in hurtful ways that cause you to shut down and feel alone.

1. They don't have enough emotional intelligence yet.

Emotional intelligence seems simple, but the art of being able to manage your own emotions while also understanding the emotions of other people in your life is hard. It's not something we are born with; it's something we learn over time.

When I joined my confessional community group of women healing together, one of the things that the psychiatrist who led our first retreat said was that we would begin to grow in our ability to care for each other's emotions well. This is the good part. The bad part is that it would become a difficult game of comparison with the other people in our lives that weren't doing this type of work. We might get irritated that they didn't respond how a woman in the group would. After all, we were essentially being trained in withness in this group. We were learning how to respond to someone who is in distress, in pain, feeling alone, or filled with shame. And that's when we saw the power of emotional intelligence.

So what do you do about that? Find people who are desiring to get better at emotional intelligence with you. Send them a copy of this book. Implement talking through emotions in your small group. And lend people grace in this area as we all lean into getting this right for each other. Also, recognize when people are *not* emotionally intelligent and curb your expectations of them.

Trying to get someone to meet your emotional needs who's not able to will always lead to disappointment. I think of it like expectations around the abilities of children. If a three-year-old kicked you in the shin (just the thought makes me cringe), you wouldn't think anything of it. Your first thought would probably be, *Where is this kid's mom?* But if a twenty-seven-year-old kicked you in the shin, you might get so mad you'd be ready to fight. It's because you expect more from a twenty-seven-year-old than you do from a three-year-old.

When we think about people who don't have the level of emotional intelligence that we really want, we have to realize that their "emotional age" may be younger than that of someone who understands how to care for us. Level setting our expectations is one way we can protect our hearts when it comes to healing in community.

2. Their own personal pain doesn't have capacity for yours.

Sometimes when people have been deeply hurt, they can become so consumed and overwhelmed with their own emotions that they can't help you process yours. They can come off as short, irritated, or zoned out when you're trying to process with them.

A good way to handle this is to ask questions on the front end about their capacity before you confide in them. You could ask, "I've got something really hard going on and would like to process it with you; do you have the capacity to chat with me about it?" Often, it's not at all about the person and their desire to care for you but everything to do with the timing of their ability to care.

There is a really interesting balance in my confessional community. When we are on our three-hour monthly call, each of us is sharing everything that's going on in our lives: the good, the bad, and everything in between. You can tell when there's someone who is able to share but not able to tend to others. And we don't hold it against them at all. Instead we honor that we are human, we each have capacity limits, and that's okay.

3. They default to spiritual bypassing.

Another reason people aren't able to hold your emotions well is because of spiritual bypassing. This is a term that was created by a psychologist named John Welwood. The main idea is that for far too long we have used spiritual practices and scriptures to put Band-Aids on emotional issues that actually need surgery in the form of mental health resources.

I believe that Jesus welcomed emotion. He didn't avoid it, go around it, or even make people think that because He was present there was no need to mourn. As a matter of fact, the Bible is crystal clear that Jesus wept over the death of a friend named Lazarus. But He didn't just cry alone, hiding His pain; He wept with His friends (John 11:34–35). He wept when Lazarus passed away, even though Jesus knew in the end He would bring him back to life. There was a moment of mourning—because Jesus' presence doesn't erase the need to mourn; it welcomes that need.

Jesus' presence doesn't erase the need to mourn; it welcomes that need.

YOU'VE BEEN HURT BY THE RESPONSES OF THOSE CLOSE TO YOU

When Mary, the sister of Lazarus, heard that Jesus was on His way, she went to Him and fell down at His feet. When He saw her tears, and those of her sister, Martha, He wept as well. It's because the God of the universe sees the tears of His people and He is moved to deep compassion. God sees our pain. God is aware of our sorrow. God remembers our tears and He is moved by them. There is no sin or shame associated with our tears; it is the way of Jesus. And if Jesus was perfect in His humanity as an example to us all, then we can feel the freedom to believe in Him and sit in our pain and emotion without using His name as a shortcut to our healing.

My encouragement to anyone who wants to offer Scripture as a means of helping someone heal is to make sure that we aren't exchanging God's witness with God's truth. Both can and should coexist. After all, Jesus was all grace and all truth, all the time.

These are just some of the problematic responses that I've mentioned and personally experienced that could make someone not want to open up again. There are more; trust me, I know. Another problematic response that I've personally experienced is when my therapist fell asleep on me—multiple times. This is what I alluded to earlier. I went to a therapist that specialized in sexual trauma after enduring infidelity and marital betrayal in 2018 and 2019, and for some reason this therapist just couldn't stay awake. Think about how hard it was for me to vulnerably share my story of repeated betrayal, thinking that I had a safe space in which to do it, only to experience what felt like abandonment by a trusted source.

The Question You Need to Ask Yourself

The question I had to ask myself is this: *Was I really going to allow one bad experience to destroy my trust in all therapists? Was I really going to short-circuit my healing process?* No. The answer will always be no. I am indebted to living a life of healing and wholeness, not only for me but for my children and the people I am in deep relationship with. I talked to my counselor about what was happening, and he was deeply sorry. He had been battling narcolepsy, and I extended grace and forgiveness while also setting a boundary that I would need to find another counselor. And my goodness, did God send me the best counselor I've ever had. She is attentive, compassionate, and professional and has gotten me through some of the darkest times.

One special moment that I had with her was the day I felt like my world was falling apart, the day my marriage actually did. One hour after receiving a call from my ex-husband confessing what he'd done, the call that exposed all of the betrayal, I had a session already scheduled with my new counselor. I remember sitting in that hotel room in Nashville in a brown leather chair pulled up to the wooden desk in my room, looking into the camera of my computer as she comforted me while I explained my disappointment with God. She didn't give me a scripture to read in that moment. She didn't give me a strategy to practice. She just sat with me and said, "Your feelings are so valid, Toni. God can handle your disappointment."

If I had let my previous bad experience with therapy stop me, I wouldn't have had those wise words spoken over me at the time I needed them the most. Here's what I know: When we are in pain, we want comfort first, not correction. We want withness, not strategy. That's the way God designed us. It's what Jesus modeled. I think it'll be extremely important to your healing journey to have people in your life who can do this well. For far too long we have gotten this wrong, and now it's time for us to get it right so that we have more people healing well and chasing after wholeness.

I know that everyone in your life may not have gotten this right. I know there's been a lot of disappointment in this area of your life. But can you hold on a little while longer? Can you pray that God begins to send people into your life who will hold your pain well? Can you set your expectations to a healthy place for people who may not be ready to hold your pain? Can you believe in people again? Can you forgive those who didn't get it right so that you can make room in your heart for those who will?

I believe you can do it. And I think your healing depends on it.

Think on This

Let's take a moment to think about the interactions that may have caused you to hesitate when it comes to opening up.

- Can you think of a time when someone responded to your pain and made it worse?
- Name two or three feelings that came up in your heart.
- Can you answer honestly if that made it difficult to trust other people with your pain?
- Can you think of one person that you can begin to rebuild trust with?

The key word in the last question is "rebuild." It isn't always easy to open up again immediately after your trust has been ruptured, but instead of focusing on opening up all the way, maybe it would be easier to focus on simply rebuilding. Step by step.

Chapter 6

YOU STRUGGLE TO BELIEVE THAT GOD NEVER LEAVES YOU

This chapter will feel like story time. It is extremely important to me that I be as open and honest with you as I am asking you to be with the people in your life. And as a Bible teacher, I want to tell stories and seeing and sharing God in them is something I want to do well. So sit back, grab your water, coffee, tea, or matcha latte, and let's find God in this story together. I think it'll be good.

It still makes me cringe a little to say I've been divorced twice by thirty-two. I still get teary. Shame still tries to come for me. I still feel like a failure some days, and I'm deeply grieved for my children daily. While my reasons for divorce were that my marriages were no longer God-honoring, and while there has been tremendous healing and freedom on the other side, it still feels like a severing—a ripping. And that ripping still hurts me more than I'd like to admit.

If one of my close friends were to ask me what my biggest feeling was in this past season, it would be crushed. I've felt crushed. You ever felt that way? Like the weightiness of this imperfect life has crushed you? Good thing for you and me Psalm 34:18 is pretty clear about God's role when we feel crushed: "The Lord is close to the brokenhearted and saves those who are crushed in spirit."

While I could've invited you into a more polished story of my life and written about only hopeful things that are all tied up in a pretty little cheerleader bow, the reason I'm sharing with you the moments in which God met me in my most difficult season is that I believe that if we are going to invite God into our healing, we need to understand His character. And His character is that of a father of children looking for protection and peace and healing. I think you see the rescuing character of God the clearest when you're lost and afraid in the valleys and He shows up right there in the hard places. After all, it's the God of Psalm 34:18 who says He's close to the brokenhearted and revives those who are crushed in spirit. It's that God that I so desperately want you to see through my stories of hope in the valleys.

If you're crushed or brokenhearted, I hope you take a moment to receive the one thing that will always be true: The God of the universe is with you. I need you to know that the God who came for me is the same God who will come for you. I am not special at all. God doesn't play favorites; He's coming for every single one of us. I promise. Let me share how I know this is true.

God Is with You

One morning I was getting ready to spend some quiet time. I usually wake up at 6:30 a.m. every day. My little son, Sammie, wakes up at seven, so I get about thirty minutes with the Lord before waking him up and then dragging my daughter, Dylan, out of bed. (She's 100 percent in the I-don't-want-to-get-up phase.) I usually spend this time in my little office nook, but on this particular day, I couldn't get out of bed. I just didn't have the strength. I did my quiet time there in my new bed bought for me by my wonderful community of friends when I moved into my new house with my children after the divorce. I grabbed my little notebook from my side table, squeezed it to my chest, and just lay there. I felt so tender that the tears seemed to come out by themselves with every blink.

The emotion that was the most present in that moment was *unwanted*. As I lay there, I realized for the first time that it had been three months since I'd been touched by another adult. And I just hated that. I hadn't been loved on. I didn't have anyone to cuddle with anymore. I was in this big old bed by myself, and I hadn't gotten a hug from a human in ninety days. (Kids don't count. Because they lick your elbows.)

I'd been processing with my counselor that I've always had this deep longing to be with a man. Even when I was a little girl and felt like my father was distant, I longed for a man to come and scoop me up, to save me. And I started to recognize a belief I've carried for years: If I don't have a man, then I am not worth anything. If I don't have a ring on my finger, then I'm not complete and God can't do His will in me.

I think it started when I was around thirteen years old. I was with a much older guy that I thought really liked me but was using me for my body. It was the last day of my freshman year in high school. My parents were out of town, and in my SpongeBob SquarePants bedroom, he took my virginity. The truth is, it was the first time that a man had really shown me attention. My dad didn't really show me attention. He never verbally said he was proud, even though he may have been. He was a very aggressive person when I was growing up and was more of the disciplinarian than my mom, which created an unhealthy fear of him and attachment to my mom. We have since redeemed our relationship, but more on that later.

So I've had this belief since I was thirteen that I'm worthless without a man. And I mean, this guy from high school was not the best guy. He cheated on me with my best friend, and I still wanted to be with him. Thankfully our relationship ended when I left my parents' house and went off to college. But then I really lost my mind and slept with so many more guys, because I was longing for attention. I was looking for deep connection, or to be honest, I was looking for my worth in men.

Fast-forward to that morning when I was lying in my bed realizing that I hadn't been cuddled or kissed or hugged or touched in three months. I was so sad because there was a part of me that believed, well, maybe I wasn't worthy to be cuddled or kissed or hugged or touched.

Here's what I wrote in my journal:

Lord, I am so deeply lonely, and I know, I know I'm not really alone. I'm actually just longing. I'm longing to be touched. I'm longing to be held. And I know that You are a father to the fatherless and a mother to the motherless, but could You also be intimate with me? Could You show me that I am actually wanted?

It feels vulnerable to share this with you.
I kept writing:

Help me believe that I'm never alone and that maybe the feelings of loneliness won't go away, but the idea that I am alone will.

And I just started weeping. I was leaning on one pillow and burying my face in another pillow as if it would stop the tears from coming. All of a sudden I felt this heat on the right side of my body. And it was like the Lord had *cuddled* me. That sounds so weird to say. I continued to cry hard, but this time the tears were different. It was as if God had swooped down into my space with me. These were tears of relief and surprise. I felt the Spirit of the Lord in my room that day, 100 percent. Can't nobody tell me nothing otherwise, okay? I have witnessed it; I have the proof in my testimony. God dwelled with me in my room that day through the power of the Holy Spirit. He comforted me.

He didn't just try to fix me, heal me, point me to Scripture in an attempt to make me more whole. He was *with* me. And I realized in that moment that every single gap, every single void, He would fill. Even the gaps of unworthiness and wanting a man to cuddle.

He won't just make you have more faith in who He is.

He won't just help you with your unbelief.

He won't just help you with your doubts about Him.

He won't just financially help you and provide for your family in all these different ways.

He won't just send friends to come for you.

The God of love, love Himself, will swoop down and come to you. He will be present, and He'll give you a hug when you need it. I received those promises that day cuddled in my bed at 6:54 a.m. And then I crawled out of bed, blew my nose, let out a big old exhale, grabbed my phone, turned my son's sound machine off, and went into mommy mode at 7:00 a.m.

Let me tell you why that moment is important today. When I felt unworthy, I knew who to go to. I didn't *need* a man to meet that longing in me; I needed my heavenly Father and then eventually His people. He's the first stop we should take. I couldn't wait to text my friends about what had happened and how God had met me. I also couldn't wait to tell my counselor that we had some work to do on this deep longing for a man to complete me. (Just kidding, I could wait. Counseling is hard, ha!)

I couldn't wait to tell my friends about this moment because I had been doing things so wrong. Let me preface what I'm getting ready to say by saying this: We will always be on a healing journey until we meet the Healer of our hearts—God Himself. Now, let's dive into Scripture.

A Rescuer to One and to All

In Matthew 18:11–13 Jesus Himself said, "What do you think? If a man owns a hundred sheep and one of them wanders away, will he not leave the ninety-nine on the hills and go to look for the one that wandered off? And if he finds it, truly I tell you, he is happier about that one sheep than about the ninety-nine that did not wander off."

Did you know that when you're the one in pain and alone and feeling abandoned and lost, Jesus' eyes are on you? I want you to think about the moment you were like that *one* sheep. The moment there was pain in your story: betrayal, lies, manipulation, abuse, abandonment, deep sorrow. And I want you to imagine being the one God comes after, leaving all of us ninety-niners on the hills living our best lives to come for you. He is coming for you. The question is, Will you let Him? Will you let Him and His people in so that you can have a better shot at healing?

When I think about this parable that Jesus shared with the disciples, I remember that moment in my bedroom. I was the

Will you let Him and His people in so that you can have a better shot at healing?

one then and I needed to be the one. I took three months off from preaching. I took a month to just be with my family and love on my kids. I was fragile and lost and betrayed. I believed in God and that He would heal me, but I was hurting, and I needed saving, and He came for me. It was God who comforted me and healed me and is healing me right now. He brought me through, and it was the ninety-nine in my army of friends and family who showed up in my life and changed everything for me, who made things a little bit lighter for me.

Our generation needs to see that He's still the God who comes for His people. He's still the God who's making ways out of no literal ways. He is still the God who makes the impossible possible. And I know that. I believe it with everything in me. Why? Because I've seen the goodness of God in the land of the living in my own life.

I believe with everything in me that no matter how painful leaving my marriage has been, and how hard a decision it was, *God rescued me.* He rescues us because He knows that we live in a dark, fallen, broken world and that we need rescue. He is always looking out into the depths, or the shallows—wherever we find ourselves—and He is ready, willing, and able to rescue us even when we don't want it. Even when we don't know we need it. He's a God of rescue. I'm hoping that something is stirring on the inside of you that refuses to heal alone. I pray that there's something in you right now that proclaims on the hills and in the valleys that goodness is coming for you too.

Think on This

Read this aloud if possible:

Lord, I know that the Bible makes it clear that You created humans and the world with good in mind. I understand that evil entered the world with Adam and Eve and now we are living in the broken in-between until we get to heaven. There are moments when it is hard to see Your goodness because of the brokenness. So would You please give me eyes to see it more clearly? Would You help me realize that no matter what sin and darkness and evil try to say or do, You remain good? Would You help me to remember that You are running after me like a good father would his lost and hurting child? Would You remind me every single day that You are the God of withness, and You're really good at it? In Jesus' name, amen.

Friend, I am believing this prayer with you. As we dive into the next section of this book, I want to remind you that you can do this. You are seen and held and chosen and safe. Hope is pumping through your veins, and your God is on the way. Let's get practical as we head into part 2.

Part 2

HOW TO BUILD A STRONG COMMUNITY

Chapter 1

UNDERSTAND ADULT FRIENDSHIP

Let me go ahead and tell you what this section of the book is *not*. It is not a transcript for a Teletubbies show where we pretend that everyone gets along and can be "besties for the restie." Friendships are hard. And relationships can be the very thing that brings the most trauma into our lives.

We aren't going to pretend that people are our savior. They sure aren't. Unlike Jesus, they did not come to this earth and live a perfect life for thirty-plus years (Hebrews 7:26). They also did not single-handedly minister to the masses, curate a discipleship team, perform thirty-seven recorded miracles, die a brutal sinner's death, predict their own death, burial, and resurrection, and then actually rise again. Your Savior is Jesus—not your bestie, or your small-group leader, or your spouse, or the CEO you want to impress, or your gym coach, or your children. Only Jesus is, and He always will be. We don't get to replace Him, even though sometimes it is way easier to put our trust in the physical presence of people over an unseen God. We just don't.

We won't put people on pedestals that we will want to rip them off of when we find out they're imperfect like we are. Again, only Jesus lived a perfect life. Our favorite pastor, worship leader, or Bible teacher has not and cannot.

And we surely aren't going to pass off our responsibility to heal on to someone else. This book is not about learning how to take our pain, traumas, griefs, and disappointments and lay them at the feet of other humans. Our healing is our responsibility, and if we are going to lay any of our brokenness down, we're going to lay it at the feet of Jesus first.

That being said, friendships and community play a vital role in our lives, starting super early.

Why Childhood Friendships Are So Important

"Do you want to be my friend?" I overheard a little girl ask her almost-new friend while I was sitting at the mall letting my son frolic in the play area. Childhood memories of the moments when it was just that easy to make friends flooded my mind. As a child I hadn't yet experienced too many hard moments with my friends and still had a pretty good view of the world. I was still in the awe-and-wonder phase of discovering the world, and shame sat in the back of my emotional and mental bus, not the

Our healing is our responsibility, and if we are going to lay any of our brokenness down, we're going to lay it at the feet of Jesus first.

driver's seat. I hadn't felt the sting of rejection enough times to take away my bravery. It was just as simple as "Do you want to be my friend?"

I watched as these girls went from strangers, to spotting each other in the play area and realizing that they were probably around the same age, to being friends in less than seven minutes. I smiled a little thinking about my own daughter, who was with her dad at the time, and how she would've totally done the same thing. Even worse, she would've given my number to a complete stranger so they could keep having playdates, because she hadn't yet needed to learn to put up boundaries for her safety.

Don't you wish making friends was that easy as an adult? Oh, but no, it's just plain old awkward for us. Here we are in line at our local grocery store and a stranger says something to us that sparks conversation. I don't know about you, but the first thing that comes to my mind is, *What am I going to say? How am I going to interface with this stranger?* Now, thankfully for me, I have tested at the highest possible number on the extrovert scale, so I get fueled by talking to people. I absolutely love it. But for anyone who is any less extroverted than I am, this could be a daunting task. Can I just say it again? Making friends as an adult is awkward. I want to lay that down in front of us so that we're all on the same page.

It's just awkward. And it's absolutely worth it.

Maybe it isn't at all about how extroverted or introverted you are. Maybe it's more about how you view yourself and the world around you. Can we get nerdy for a second again? I want to unpack what it means to be aware of our childhoods and the way we interfaced with the people around us as little kids and how that impacts all of us now. Then I'll give you five ways to find friends around you. Deal? Let's go! Through work with my therapist and lots of reading on parenting and trauma, I've learned that childhood friendships can play a huge role in shaping our social skills, self-esteem, and overall emotional development. Our early relationships lay the foundation for how we form and maintain friendships in adulthood. It's just the way we are wired. The impact of these friendships can be seen in lots of important areas.

1. Social Skills Development

Childhood friendships are often our first experience with social interactions outside of our family. These early relationships teach us how to communicate, share, and resolve conflicts. Through play and conversation, as children we learn essential social skills like empathy, cooperation, and negotiation. These types of skills are vital for forming healthy adult relationships.

Here's an example: A child who learns to effectively communicate her needs and listen to others is more likely to have successful and fulfilling friendships later in life. Because I grew up in a household where we didn't talk about our emotions or communicate with each other through conflict, I had to learn how to manage healthy communication as an adult through other means, like counseling and trial and error. It has been especially difficult for me to communicate my needs in friendships and relationships, making them feel one-sided and lonely when the problem was only a matter of healthy communication. See how important that is?

2. Self-Esteem

The quality of our childhood friendships can significantly influence our self-esteem and self-concept. It's not about how many people are in our lives; it's about our need for good, positive friendships, the kind that make kids feel accepted and valued, and increase their self-confidence and sense of belonging.

On the flip side, negative experiences, like bullying or exclusion, can lead to feelings of inadequacy and low self-worth. If you struggled as a teen with not being invited to the "cool kids" table, you may end up fighting as an adult to be seen in spaces where you feel important. All of our early experiences really do shape how we view ourselves and how we expect others to treat us in adulthood. Adults with positive childhood friendships have a more secure sense of themselves, making it much easier for them to form and maintain healthy relationships. And isn't that what we all want? Relationships that are healthy?

3. Attachment Styles

This is currently a buzzy term on the internet! Childhood friendships also interact with our attachment styles, which are first formed in our relationships with our primary caregivers. Children who are securely attached and feel safe, supported, and seen are more likely to form stable and trusting friendships when they're older. In contrast, children with insecure attachment styles could really struggle with trust and intimacy in their friendships. And we absolutely need trust and intimacy to build healthy relationships with those around us.

Our attachment styles leak over into adulthood, and they influence how we approach and manage our relationships. Securely attached adults are typically more comfortable with closeness and independence in their friendships, but those with insecure attachment styles may experience anxiety or avoidance in their social interactions. This is why we get into counseling and heal. Because who wants to bring an unhealthy attachment style from their past into their future?

4. Coping Mechanisms and Emotional Regulation

The truth is, in childhood, friendships provide a crucial context for developing coping mechanisms and emotional regulation strategies. When we interact with our friends, we learn how to manage our emotions, ask for support, and cope with stress. Our early experiences shape our emotional resilience and how we handle challenges in our adult relationships. Adults who had supportive friendships or parental relationships in childhood can successfully navigate conflicts and stress in their adult friendships. Because the adults in my life raised their voices when I was little, it's very difficult for me to regulate when someone raises their voice at me now. The wounds we develop as children, if left unhealed, will become adult wounds.

5. Expectations and Patterns

Our early friendships create expectations and patterns that we carry into adulthood. For example, a child who received consistent support and loyalty from friends is likely to expect and seek out those same qualities in their adult relationships. On the flip side, a child who experienced betrayal or inconsistency could struggle with trust and have a real fear around abandonment in their adult friendships. All of these patterns can be deeply ingrained, influencing our choice of friends and how we interact with them. We attract what we expect.

In a nutshell, the friendships we form in childhood have a lasting impact on our adult relationships. They shape our social skills, self-esteem, attachment styles, coping mechanisms, and expectations. Everything! Being able to understand the influence of our early experiences can help us recognize patterns in our adult friendships and work toward healthier, more fulfilling relationships, leading us to feeling safe enough to heal with our people. As we reflect on our childhood friendships, we can gain insight around our behavior and make conscious efforts to improve our social connections. Whether through therapy, self-reflection, or intentional relationship building, acknowledging and addressing the impact of our early friendships can lead to more meaningful and supportive adult relationships.

How to Find the Friends You Need

Start asking yourself questions like these:

- What friendship when I was a child is influencing how I view friends right now?
- Is there a reason I don't have any friendships left from my childhood?
- What triggers me in my friendships today that I can trace back to my childhood or teenage years?

For me, I think back to how many organizations and extracurricular activities I was in growing up, from cheerleading in school to competitive cheer outside of school to drama club and thespian society to debate team and even the step team. I was involved in all the things. Which meant I also had multiple friend groups all the time. I became a little chameleon, shapeshifting to fit in and activating the people pleaser that was in me. I didn't settle into friendships, because it always felt like I would be hopping into a new group anyway. I didn't go deep at all.

I remember when I realized that I still do this as an adult. Going deep with no one but befriending everyone. And while it's a beautiful thing to be inviting and extroverted, connecting with as many people as possible, I also realized that I had to balance going deep with a few and managing the social butterfly part of me too. I wasn't being deeply seen by anyone; instead I was managing schedules and hangs. So I decided to join my confessional community, and that meant fewer people to go deep with. I chose to break the cycle of surface-level fun and submitted myself to what it means to bring a few close.

It was perfect for me. It changed me. It healed me. And

while I still invite everyone from my local gym, even those whose names I don't know, to girls' nights, spades nights at my house, and park days for our children, I know where home base is. I know that when temptation comes or darkness tries to creep into my healing journey, there are six women and a group text waiting for me to go deep.

I know it may not be the easiest thing for you to find, so I've put together some practical ways to find friends. My hope is that as you cultivate simple friendships and relationships, God will impress on your heart those that you can really go deep with. It'll be worth it.

Have I already mentioned this wouldn't be easy? Just a reminder that it's not! I'm a no-fluff type of girl; you know that by now. However, I believe that this list, the guidance you've received from reading this book, and prayer to a God who cares about you and your friendships will help tremendously as you fight to never heal alone. Here we go.

Join support groups or healing circles.

This was super huge for me as I was walking through a journey of healing from betrayal and sexual trauma in 2019. A few of my friends knew what was happening in my marriage and referred me to an amazing psychologist who specialized in betrayal and sexual trauma. I wanted to fight to rebuild my trust in my marriage and really heal from everything that had happened, in hopes that we would make it and I would be able to trust again.

I started meeting with a psychologist, and my eyes were

opened to how truly deep my sexual trauma went, even into childhood. A few sessions in, he recommended I take a look at the upcoming therapy group that focused on women who'd been walking through some of the same things I was. At first I was like, *Umm, complete strangers finding out about what's going on in my marriage? But I'm in ministry. I stand on platforms. What if someone recognizes me?* None of it mattered. Healing plays no favorites. And I wanted healing more than anything.

I dove in, and every Tuesday for sixteen weeks I met with other women who would bravely share some really hard parts of their stories. We were complete strangers, and yet we deeply connected to each other through our pain. My heart and mind completely transformed. This was before I joined my confessional community, and I think the Lord was preparing me for what it looks like to heal around a circle. I want to encourage you to look for local or online support groups focused on healing, whether it's for mental health, grief, addiction recovery, or other areas of personal growth. You can even ask your current counseling center if they have or know of any. These groups provide a safe space to share experiences and connect with others on a similar journey. They have the power to absolutely change you.

Attend workshops and retreats.

Have you ever heard of the phrase "continuing education"? Well, let's make a new one: "continuing healing"! I think you know that we'll never arrive at "all done healing" on this earth. We will be healing for the rest of our time here. So continuing to heal is something we have to commit to. I've been on my healing journey at this point for nine years. I've had four different counselors, I've gotten certifications around healing, done multiple intensives and retreats, and I am completely open to doing more. By finding and diving into workshops and retreats, I've ended up in places with women with similar stories to mine and, even better, similar mindsets when it comes to healing.

These environments often create deep connections, as we are all sharing a transformative experience together. When you're able to connect deeply through pain, it changes you. I experienced this going to Lysa TerKeurst's Haven Place Retreat in North Carolina. It was for women processing through betrayal trauma, who were figuring out if our marriages or relationships were still God-honoring and what kinds of boundaries we needed to set up, or if we needed to say goodbye. These things are transformational!

Volunteer for causes you care about.

I get to volunteer at a wonderful shelter in Atlanta for women who have been through trauma and abuse. Not only does this help to bring people into my life that care about the causes and people that I care about, but it also gives my pain a sense of meaning and purpose. (We'll talk more about that in another chapter.) I want to encourage you to engage in volunteer work for causes that resonate with you and, on the way, pray that God would connect you with people who are just as passionate as you with whom you can develop a relationship outside of serving.

Take classes or join clubs.

This one is my favorite! Joining Burn Boot Camp, a CrossFit-style gym with the most intentional community, was the smartest decision I've made in my thirties! While I originally went to become healthier physically and mentally, socially the gym has been the best for connecting with people I never would've met otherwise.

Maybe for you it's the gym, a local family club, golf, tennis, the mall, pottery, a play place that has memberships for moms and their kids to meet other moms, a book club, art classes, hiking or running groups, or cooking workshops. Whatever it is, get out of your comfort zone, dive right in, and allow yourself to have some fun meeting people no matter what stage of life you're in. Shared interests provide a natural foundation for building friendships.

Use social media and online communities.

Okay, this can be a weird one for many of us. Meeting strangers online can be downright awkward, yet it can also lead to some incredible real-life connections. Most of the people I know who are in my line of work are people I originally met online as Instagram friends. Then we end up at the same conference or in the same city for a networking opportunity or church speaking engagement, and next thing you know, a whole new authentic, connected relationship is formed!

Utilize social media platforms and online communities to connect with others. There are lots of groups on Facebook, Meetup, and other platforms where you can find people with similar interests and life experiences, including those focused on healing and personal growth.

Attend a church and join a small group.

Just typing these words brought up some heartache from bad experiences with people in the church. I've been hurt not only by people in the church but by people on social media, at the gym, at workshops and retreats. And if I am willing to give those arenas another chance, I for sure should be willing to give God's people another chance too.

The church was designed for this very reason—to connect believers to one another for the sake of the gospel, to look more like Jesus, and to treat more people like He did as well. The church is the hospital for our souls and every other aspect of our healing journey. But attending a church isn't the key to deeper relationships. I've held on to this statement since I worked at North Point Ministries under the leadership of Andy Stanley: "Life change happens in circles, not rows." This is the truth. We digest a thirty-to-forty-five-minute message in rows. We lift our hands in holy communion with God in rows. But we change deeply when we are eye to eye and shoulder to shoulder. We change in the presence of safe people, who create safe spaces.

So yes, joining a church can build your relationship with God, but forming a circle (small group) is what builds your relationship with God's people. Give it another try, be intentional about connecting beyond Sunday morning, and pray for God to meet you through His people.

UNDERSTAND ADULT FRIENDSHIP

I hope these ideas help you build meaningful connections that support your healing journey. I want to encourage you to mark these pages and come back to these ideas again and again. You deserve it. Your heart deserves it. And you have to do your work. We will drift toward isolation when we are in our deepest pain, but we have to fight against the drift. We have to walk into the light and look for where God's people are. And prepare for things not to work. For someone to be weird, for it not to be a good fit. Transition from those you don't connect deeply with in a kind and honoring way, put your social hat back on, and dive in again. "Do you want to be my friend?" doesn't just belong to the little girls of this world; it belongs to the little girls who are still inside us longing for connection, longing to be seen across the room. As my girl Jennie Allen says, it's time to go "find your people." Your healing depends on it. And as you're finding your people, it's helpful to keep in mind a few good characteristics to look for.

Think on This

Grab a pen and paper or open the notes app in your phone and complete the following:

- Create a list of three to five places that you *have* been before where you think you'll be able to find friends.
- Create a list of three to five places that you *haven't* been before where you think you'll be able to find friends.
- Create a list of three conversation starters that will hopefully lead to a new connection with a new friend.

Bonus: If you have been hurt by someone in the church, create a list of three churches that you would like to visit, and pray about sharing your story of hurt with someone there.

Chapter 8

LOOK FOR THE CHARACTERISTICS OF A GOOD FRIEND

Here's the truth that I will shout from the rooftops: *We need to heal in community.* Here's the other truth: *We need said community to be healthy.* It's not enough for us to have people in our lives. We need people who are healthy and honest and challenge us and point us to Jesus and speak life into us. We need certain types of people who can carry the weight of healing.

When I really accepted this, I was kind of mad. I kept thinking, *You mean to tell me I have to overcome the awkwardness that is finding a friend as an adult? I mean, have you tried to engage with someone as an adult to be your friend? Like, what do you even say?* "Hey, love those tennis shoes." "What do you do?" "Do you like groceries and kids?" "DO YOU WANT TO BE MY FRIEND?" Awkward to say the least, right?

Well, not only do we have to open ourselves up, but we also have to be honest about the characteristics of a good friend and what we need so that we are able to invite people into our lives that are actually healthy for us. And even more important than a good friend is a godly friend. The truth is, the world views friendship much differently than God does. And it is up to us to have a biblical filter when it comes to choosing good friends. But don't you worry, *I got you*!

The Five Characteristics of a Good and Godly Friend

We're going to dive into a few of the characteristics that will let you know that you've got a good and godly friend on your hands. Get out your notes, highlighters, book stickies, and such. Let's go deep!

1. They are authentic.

Authenticity is huge. Some people call it being "real," but let's call it for what it is and use language that'll help us identify who should be in our lives. Authentic friends aren't in the relationship for what they can get out of it, and they do not abandon their people in bad times. They stay. They get honest. They say the hard things and they don't let shame drive the friendship bus. Because they know that friendship isn't all about them; it's about showing up for someone else. And as you show up for them and they show up for you, the friendship flourishes. Let Proverbs 17:17 guide you: "A friend loves at all times, and a brother is born for adversity."

Friendship isn't about hanging out with someone who has lots in common with you at a cute little swanky coffee shop with eight-dollar lattes. (And I love me some cute little swanky coffee shops.) But come on, you can find a complete stranger who has lots in common with you over a latte. These things don't define a good friend. God clearly defines a good friend for us in the Bible:

- A good godly friend stays loyal and helpful in times of need. (Proverbs 17:17)
- A good godly friend tells you the whole truth even if it stings a little. (Psalm 15:2–4)
- A good godly friend not only tells you the truth but they also do it with grace and kindness. (Ephesians 4:29)
- A good godly friend loves well. They love like Jesus would. (1 Corinthians 13)
- (Okay, this one is a little wild.) If needed, a good godly friend should be willing to give up their life for you. (John 15:13)

How are you feeling about the lineup of your current friends? Do they practice some of these? None? One or two? Or if you don't have friends for whatever reason, do you believe that you're worthy of friends that have these traits? For some of us, it's hard to find friends like this because we don't think we deserve it. Maybe our own family hasn't treated us this way, so we are conditioned to settling for less than what we need.

Let me be the first to say it clearly: You are worthy of good godly friends. You are worthy of people who are loyal to you and don't abandon you. You are worthy of people who tell you the truth because they care about your soul more than your comfort. You are worthy to be talked to with kindness and dignity. You are worthy of biblical love, especially when you are hurting. You are worthy to have someone stand in front of you when danger comes your way and shield you. You are worthy of someone who shows you their authentic self. And you are capable of being this type of friend too. I won't go deep into this now, but I want to be clear that healthy community goes both ways—others doing their work to show up for you and you doing yours too.

2. They tell you the whole truth, even if it stings, with grace and kindness.

Let me tell you what's not fun all the time: being divorced twice, with two children, a public platform, and a wildly busy life. I have found myself single in my thirties, "dating" Jesus and worrying about what life will look like over the years when it comes to love and relationships. I am grateful for my life, and I am grieved over all that this life has cost me. I texted a good friend named Esther about this, and here's how it all went down:

> **Me:** My frand. Listen, I love you! And I need some help as a single woman out here. How are we not having sex? How

LOOK FOR THE CHARACTERISTICS OF A GOOD FRIEND

are we finding good, godly men? Someone send me the playbook. Because I'm being flirted with so hard and I'm like . . .

Esther: Girl, welcome to the reality. We do our best fam, that's what we do.

Me: I just don't even know what to do. If I go on a date, am I gonna do something I'll regret? I'm scared. I haven't dated in so long.

Esther: First, who are you going on a date with? Second, whenever you have time to chat, I have all the stories. The good times, the bad dates, and healing moments in between. And I will share anything with you that you ask. Open book over here, my gal!

Me: Okay, so I don't know if I'll ever go on a date or not. I was never asked out when I was young. I just had sex with random guys, then married two guys really fast without consulting God. I even talked to my counselor about it. I'm just so scared.

Esther: The great thing you have already done is you already became vulnerable and started healing before your divorce. You already have that working in your favor. You're not the same college Toni. This ends well for you. Better than you expected. I love you. Your wildness is a gift from God; don't let the enemy make you think it's a liability when it's not. It just needs to be handled carefully in this season! And that's why you got a tribe around you that is gonna cheer you on while you find out how to walk uncaged. Freedom is scary when you've been trapped for years, but you have us! And we gonna keep you on your feet!

Here's what I loved so much about this conversation and many other conversations with Esther: She's not afraid to go first. She's been through hard stuff. Divorce, public humiliation, figuring out dating again, ministry life, all the things. And instead of hiding her suck, she willingly chooses to share her pain so people like me who are coming behind her can experience an easier path.

Look for the people who are willing to go first. Who are willing to share openly from a place of hope. Because let me tell you, the friends that are sharing only from a place of bitterness aren't the ones you want when you're up against pain and heartache. You need some hopeful people in your life! The rule of thumb around sharing your pain that I practice is that if you're not hopeful about it, don't share it. Just wait until you heal some more. You want friends who are practicing this so that they can inspire you, not hinder you. You want people who say, "I'll be with you in the valleys, but I won't leave you there. Let's claw our way out of the valleys of despair and get to mountains of hope!" That's the kind of friend we want on the bus, isn't it?

3. They have been through hard things, and they also get your thing.

Another little cherry on top that I realized in my conversations with Esther, as well as other women like my best friends Eryn and Jamie, is that they get *my* thing. They share common pain with me. I say this is a cherry on top because it's not a nonnegotiable. But it is extremely helpful to have someone who understands your pain because they recognize it from their own story. This is also why I think it's important to get into group therapy or group intensives with a specific topic of pain if possible. Being in a circle of women who can look me in the eye and cry the same tears while being guided by a professional counselor who's specializing in our specific pain is something that has helped me heal tremendously.

If you're divorced, finding someone who's gone through divorce is helpful.

If you've endured infertility, finding women and men who are enduring it or have endured it is helpful.

If you've had tension with your family, maybe your parents, finding someone who's learned how to place healthy boundaries while honoring their parents as the Bible instructs is helpful.

If you've battled with body-image issues or an eating disorder, finding someone who's developed a healthy relationship with their body is helpful.

If you've been single for longer than your heart wants and you're trying to honor God in the waiting, finding someone who's done that well is helpful.

Someone who gets *your* thing can speak to *your* thing, and I believe it makes healing from *your* thing so much easier.

4. They love like Jesus.

I was recently at a wedding for a good friend who'd gone through a terrible divorce, spent years single, dating, not dating, and longing to be remarried. She met the sweetest guy named Tyler, who was a single dad with two daughters. He'd gone through a very hard divorce as well and was now raising these sweet girls on his own. The wedding was a real tearjerker, let me just say that.

One of the moments that really did my heart some good was when the groom's cousin came up to give his toast. He started off by explaining that he had been living life on the edge. Gambling and drinking, he owed money to Tyler's dad, his uncle, and he just couldn't seem to get his ducks in a row. He ended up having to move in with Tyler and his parents, and Tyler invited him to a youth conference. There he was, a grown man, a gambler, a liar—and Tyler didn't think twice about inviting him to the conference.

He got a little choked up sharing the next part, and so did everyone else in the room. He took a deep breath and said, "Tyler loved me like Jesus would. He didn't judge me, he invited me to a sacred space, he believed in the good in me. And that night, at that youth conference (as a grown man, ha!), I fell in love with Jesus. Because Tyler showed me what Jesus really looks like. And it changed my whole entire life."

Good godly friends are redemptive in nature. They are like Jesus, who loves us despite us. Who keeps inviting us to sacred spaces with Him. Who plays no favorites. Who is all grace, all truth, all the time.

5. You can be vulnerable with them.

Lastly, we get to become vulnerable with our trusted people. This is where you'll really begin to see lasting change. Once we are honest with ourselves, and then with God, we have strengthened our emotional muscle enough to do the same in real-life community with people. This is a war tactic! We rob the enemy of his power because we flick on the light. His real strength is in the darkness, and when his punk self is exposed to the light, he loses his strength. ("Punk" was a little aggressive of me, but we're gonna keep it moving here.) He can no longer scare us. He can no longer keep us in the bondage of hiding. When our story sees the light, the dark parts of it start to see the real grace and power of a God who redeems. I've seen how being vulnerable can lead to great community in my own life in so many ways.

I live on a hill with my kiddos. But not like a little baby hill that's kind of cute. You have to drive across a bridge, go up half the hill, cut a quick left, and brave the rest of the hill. It's one of those hills where if you park on it, you better watch out for the door because gravity will undoubtedly try to smoosh you in it.

Long story short, I live on a giant hill.

So everything I do, from making sure my two-year-old son doesn't tumble down it, to yard work, to Christmas decorations and deliveries, is an iron-man sport. I don't really mind it because the hill sets our house into a little corner in nature, which is my favorite thing about it. You know what my least favorite thing about it is though? The trash. The garbage truck can't make it up the hill, so every Monday night I have to drag my two large, very full trash and recycling bins down that giant hill.

I don't hate much in this world. I don't even say the word "hate" often. But I hate, hate, hate taking those trash bins down that giant hill every week. Not to fret—after a month of taking them down I realized that a better idea would be to leave the trash bins next to my mailbox at the bottom of the hill in the cul-de-sac and just drive our trash down and pop it right on inside. I'd figured it out. I had done it. I had conquered the hill and those disrespectful trash bins!

Until . . .

My sweet neighbor told my landlord that he would prefer I bring the bins up every week. As a new single mom trying to figure out life and healing and career and parenting and finances on my own, I was crushed. It was a small thing, but it was one hard thing that I didn't love that I had taken off my plate, and now it was back on the plate staring at me every single week. There was also something about a man who probably didn't understand the emotional and physical toll this was having on me that made it sting a little more.

Monday night came. The trash bins were so full. I put my tennis shoes on, grabbed the handles of the trash bins, tilted them just right, and started making the trek down the hill. I felt the lump come up. Slowly but surely the tears welled up and I was full-blown dragging and crying and balancing and stopping so the trash wouldn't fall out. The truth is, when I was married, I would have to take out the trash anyway, but I think the fact that I *had* to do it now was really hard to accept. It was so hard, and it was all my responsibility. No one was coming for me. This was my house, my trash, my gigantic trash bins, my huge hill. I thought no one was coming for me, until I posted this caption on Instagram:

It shocked me that pulling up our trash bins would be triggering for me this morning. I mean, I'd always taken the trash out, even when I was married, but there's something about *having* to do it that really got me. I think it was the reminder that I am a single mom, responsible for 3 humans, a house, two cars, finances, and so much more. I'm the covering of our family and I wasn't designed or created to be and so this sucks . . . *and* (not but) God is still a gap-filling God, a protector, and the head of my life. He's with me and you in the hard, and sucky, and smelly parts of our lives. I think that's good news.

Then two guys from my gym, a dear worship leader friend, and my bestie's husband messaged me and asked if they could come a week or two out of the month and bring my trash bins down. I was vulnerable about my feelings, and they came for me because that's what good friends do. They show up, they protect, they take big trash bins down big hills—they help.

Here's the truth that you may not want to hear: To find people who understand your story, you're going to have to share your story. I know, vulnerability is like a gold-plated bracelet. It's real cute and shiny on the outside, but that thing will turn your wrist green once the shiny stuff fades away. People love the word "vulnerability," and we even want people in our lives who are vulnerable. But when it comes to actually practicing vulnerability, it gets scary and real hard. I'm telling you, your story can only be healed in the light. And if you're going to press into this healing-in-community thing, you're going to have to get

To find people who understand your story, you're going to have to share your story.

good at *doing* community. One of the ways to *do* community well is to be open and honest so that your people are connecting with the real version of you and not the mannequin that you're hiding behind.

My life verse, 2 Corinthians 12:9, has been a wakeup call toward vulnerability I didn't know I needed. The apostle Paul wrote that God's power is made perfect in our weakness. To God Himself, our real power and strength are found in our ability to embrace vulnerability, to be weak and honest about it. And the first step to this is being willing to be honest with ourselves. We have to acknowledge the truth of the pain in our stories instead of numbing it, sweeping it under a rug, and hiding our stories. I know it's uncomfortable, I know it makes you feel weak (and not in the good way that invites God's power in), but it's so necessary. Once we are honest with ourselves about the pain in our stories, then we will be able to be honest with God.

Typically, when we try to handle our pain without God, it becomes big enough to consume us. But when we get to a place where we can be honest with God, we begin to flex the spiritual muscle of surrender like we're at the gym (one of my favorite places to be). After my second divorce I'd gotten such bad anxiety I wasn't eating or sleeping well, and I became really weak. I wasn't able to carry my one-year-old son up the stairs without running out of breath and taking breaks—lots of breaks. When he wanted me to rock him to sleep, I couldn't stand. I had to sit and rock him in a chair.

I started to try to strengthen my body by going to the gym—and I went especially hard on arm days. Now? I'm able to do a push-up with my ten-year-old daughter on my back and I can hold my boy for way longer periods at a time. My consistency at the gym helped me to become stronger to care for the people that I care most about. Your consistency at being open and honest, practicing vulnerability, will help you become stronger to care for the fragile parts of your story. Meet with God consistently. Show up and give Him your honesty.

God has a plan to bring you back to His goodness.

How do I know? I know because *I have witnessed it*. I've witnessed it in my own heart, in my honesty with God, and with the people in my life who have met me at the mile markers of this marathon called life and said, "Don't give up, Toni. Imagine you're at mile twenty-five of a twenty-six-mile marathon. You've just got one mile left, baby girl. Hold on." (Thanks, Melissa!)

Now I get to say the same to you. I know it's hard, I know your legs feel heavy, I know you've been hurt, I know it's hard to trust again. Hold on. You can make the last mile. You can do the hard thing. You can trust again; I know you can. I believe in you. But way more important than my belief in you, I believe in a God who will carry you the rest of the way if you need it. Let Him carry you.

Think on This

- Can you list a friend or two who already has the characteristics of a godly friend? Start praying

LOOK FOR THE CHARACTERISTICS OF A GOOD FRIEND

about deepening your relationship with them. Can you get vulnerable with them about one hard thing you're going through now?
- Do you know of anyone you haven't befriended who has the characteristics of a godly friend? Start praying about the conversation starters you created and how you can use them with this person.

Chapter 9

FIND THE RIGHT PLAYERS FOR YOUR TEAM

I will always be healing from the brokenness of this world, and so will you. We will never arrive at "all better" on this earth. However, along the way, we can gain wisdom that can be shared. Not from doing it all perfectly but often from doing it wrong. Friend, I have the authority to say what I am getting ready to say, because I have done some things so very wrong and it cost me so much. I haven't shared the details of this part of my story until now, but I feel I'm ready and that God will use it to help you.

After my first divorce, I was very fragile. Years of verbal abuse, fighting, serving under toxic church leadership, barely making ends meet. I'd never gone to counseling, I wasn't intentional about community, I still battled with alcohol and drugs to numb the pain of my marriage and the abuse of my past as a little girl, all while trying to balance ministry. It wasn't a good situation.

Once I left the marriage, not much changed. I was living with another single mom, looking for a job, and I met a guy at a meeting for a ministry project I was consulting. He was extremely assertive, reminded me of my dad, was a leader in the church, and was someone I really thought I could trust. Fast-forward five months and we were married. I know, it feels cringe to even say out loud. I was desperate, broken, broke, lonely, unhealthy, and alone. I barely talked about him to the few friends I still had. I didn't tell my parents. I didn't have a counselor to tell. I only had my own judgment, and my judgment was fragmented and needed years of healing and accountability to be able to make this decision. I chose to heal and do life alone and it cost me years of heartache and trauma. And not only me—eventually my daughter.

Once in the marriage, I realized it was another really toxic situation and I couldn't get out. I was afraid and embarrassed to get another divorce, especially after hiding this new marriage from my parents and friends in the first place. I believed in us and really thought this was my shot at redemption. I think sometimes we want redemption so bad, we'll try to create it for ourselves as if that's not God's job.

You know the end of this story. I ended up with another divorce anyway, but this time things are much different. This time I have an army. God is the General, and I've got my counselor as a frontline soldier and a whole division of God-fearing, wise women leading me every step of the way. And here's what's more beautiful than having these people in my life right now: I've had them for the past five years. While I was still in my second marriage, I got into counseling, did multiple rounds of trauma treatment, invested in intensives, read books, and listened to podcasts on healing. I became as much of an expert as I could in what it looks like to heal and chase after wholeness no matter how bad it hurt. I knew that not healing alone would be the best way to face life's valleys.

This was God's way—and it worked. I actually think that choosing to start healing in the presence of God and His people while still married gave me eyes to see that my marriage was no longer God-honoring. I think it gave me the foundational courage to leave when I discovered more betrayal. And it was the army of wise women I had in front of me that reminded me that leaving this time was the right decision. They held me accountable even when that thirteen-year-old girl in me wanted to stay in the chaos because it was familiar. But not more familiar than the life of healing I'd built for me and my children. This time chaos wasn't the answer; this time it was peace.

Do you have people that will help you choose peace over chaos? Do you have people that will be with you while you cry, and also wipe your tears and give you a pep talk toward healing? That's what my friends Jamie and Lisa and Jo and Eryn did for me. Do you have someone who will sit on the phone and listen to you cry a guttural cry? One who comes from a deeply broken heart?

Here's where this will get hard. You may be tempted to fall

into the pain-comparison trap right here. Maybe you and your father or mother or friend haven't reconciled. Maybe you're still in that abusive or toxic marriage. Maybe you don't have a team that will support you during a painful transition out. Now is the time to change that. Got your notes and pen? Let's dive in.

Right Person, Right Place, Right Time

The greatest leadership lesson I've ever learned was from a faithful leader and pastor named Jeff. I was sitting in a creative meeting with him and other staff members at our church planning out our creative messaging for the next few Sundays when he started talking about how good leaders build great teams.

But first, I want to make it clear that we are all leading something, whether it be our children, our college team, our company, our department at work, or our small group from church. Leadership is something that we all have stakes in. And as we are diving into what it looks like to have deep community and stop hiding, we also get to lead our healing journeys. We are the creative directors over our strategy to heal.

When I talk about leadership in this chapter, I want to make sure you don't discount yourself in it. You are leading something that could change the way you see yourself, the way you interact with people, the way you trust again, the way you manage pain, and the way you get back up and fight the good fight on this earth. With that being said, imagine yourself at this creative meeting learning one of the greatest leadership lessons ever, one that will hopefully make you a better leader, as it did for me.

So Jeff was talking about building a great team. And he said that it only happens when you get serious about bringing the right people on the bus. A staff member asked, "But how do you make sure you've got the right people on the bus?"

Jeff replied, "Use the three R's strategy: right person, right place, right timing." *Mind blown.* It was simple. Building the right team was about making sure they were the right people for the right place or position and that the timing was right. And if one or two out of the three didn't feel right, it was a no! If three out of the three don't feel right, you guessed it—big fat no. But the real key that Jeff later unpacked for us was understanding that this was an overarching idea or strategy that should be applied on a very individual level. Each person had to be filtered through the three R's. Each person had to be right for the culture of the organization; each person had to be in their right place with the right gifting to carry out their role. And each person had to be ready in the moment to fulfill their role well.

Here's what's fun. This applies not just to organizations, churches, and sports teams but also to your community "team." Each person that you choose to bring on your healing journey should be carefully examined and prayed about. I know, this thing is getting intense! But healing is intense! The pain we have to be honest about, the childhood wounds we have to hold, the temptations we have to manage, the accountability we need to put in place, the behaviors we have to learn and relearn—I mean, it's a full-on sport. (See what I did there?) So you're going to need to build a team. And the truth is, it may take more than one or two people.

Why? Because we are all unique and bring our different skill sets to the table. We have friends who give us confidence, ones who are good for just listening, ones who bring us to church and point us back to Jesus (hopefully all of them do that, but you know there's always that one who will be prostrate in her room praying the walls down or sprinkling holy oil all over everything), and maybe ones who don't have the emotional capacity to be there for you but show up in other ways. That's why teams are good. Because when we get the right people, in their rightful places, in the right timing, we're covered on all sides.

After my family fell apart, the Lord blessed me and my two kids and our au pair (our live-in nanny) with a beautiful rental home. And it was insane how it all went down. When I realized I needed to be in a safer space with my children, I called my friend Jen who works in real estate. By the next day she'd put together some housing options for us. I went to the first house on the list with my friend Belinda on a Friday, and we both felt it. This was our house. I emailed the Realtor and let her know I'd filled out the application and was ready if the landlord approved. The next day the lease was in my email inbox at 1:00 p.m. She had already set up a meeting with the landlord, who'd just recently returned from his honeymoon. He was marrying a woman who had been a single mom for seven years, and they felt compelled to give the house to us—at a lower rate than what the original listing was for. *I call that a God wink.*

Once we all got settled and I had taken some much-needed time away from ministry to heal, I took my first work trip since everything had happened. Anna Julia, our au pair, was

When we get the right people, in their rightful places, in the right timing, we're covered on all sides.

home with the kids. I was sitting in the greenroom after recording something for an organization called MOPS (Moms of Preschoolers) when Anna Julia texted me one word: *Toni*.

We have since discussed what it is like to work for someone with anxiety. When someone texts me just my name, I assume someone has died and my brain beelines to all the worst thoughts, which then sends me into a panic attack.

So of course I started freaking out. Then Anna Julia sent me a video of our beautiful new home . . . flooding. It had gotten super cold in Atlanta and a pipe had burst, and my son was doing the worm in the water. It was like the Splashtown wave pool. If you are from Texas, you know exactly what the Splashtown wave pool is. He was swimming in the living room. My au pair was freaking out.

But when I saw what was happening, somehow I was calm. I was calm because I'd already been through a lot, and I'd seen God come through for me. It's just what He does. My faith was activated, because I knew He'd come through.

Friend, what's so powerful about our faith is our *remembrance*. When something bad happens, we can say, "He did it before. He's not going to let me down." He is a good God who comes for us. And He turns all the bad, sucky, treacherous, horrible, terrible things into good things because He's a good God and He loves us. And sometimes He shows His love through other people. *This is about to get good.*

The MOPS team that had invited me was watching me on that call with Anna.

"Are you okay?" they queried. "What's going on?"

"My house is flooded. All of it. It's just flooded."

"Are you okay?" they asked in unison.

"God's going to fix it," I assured them.

Looking back on that moment, I may have seemed like a real psychopath. "He's going to do it," I repeated.

Returning to my phone call with Anna Julia, I coached her, "Hey, you just calm down. I'll call the landlord. It's okay."

I called the landlord. I enlisted my neighbor Mike. Then I called my good friends Belinda and Terrence, telling them I didn't know what to do.

"This is crazy," Belinda said. "We actually have a water vac because our basement flooded a month or two ago." She and Terrence came over and cleaned it up.

When my landlord came over to evaluate, he let me know that this had happened before. And he suspected there was a problem with that specific pipe. Because he'd had to rip up all the flooring the last time, he knew it would be a pretty long process. He also knew that the water wasn't coming from the floor; it was likely coming from the walls, so they'd probably have to rip out the walls. And then redo the walls. And then repaint the walls.

It. Was. Madness.

And I don't know why, but I was fine. I was calm. I knew that God was going to make it right. I believe that when God brings us to a Red Sea in our lives, His intent is always to part it. And He is not going to bring us all the way through escape, through rescue, to the Red Sea, and promise to part it without parting it. He is going to blow our minds. Pain, adversity, getting through it with God is our guarantee that on the other side of it, it's going to be good. It's going to be better. It's going to be better because He's going to be glorified in it.

I called my friend Jen in real estate who had helped us get the house. She had a condo close by and traveled frequently.

"Jen," I began when she answered the phone, "I hope that you're not home. Ha! It's not something I'd normally say, but me and the kids and Anna need a place to stay."

"Girl," she assured me, "I'm not home for a couple weeks. Go ahead—do it." So I packed everything up and planned on taking the family first thing in the morning.

When my landlord brought the water retention people, he explained, "They're going to test the floors for the moisture and all the things."

"Cool, no problem." I went upstairs to give Sammie a bath, and when I put him to bed and came back downstairs, my landlord was standing there, looking around, scratching his head. And the whole team of five water retention workers was there with him.

"Toni," the landlord said, "this is unheard of. They can't find the moisture."

One of the workers asked, "Can you tell us? Can you show us where the water was?"

I didn't hesitate. "Everywhere. It was everywhere. The whole thing was wet."

They couldn't find moisture anywhere. I watched them take more readings, and the house was as dry as if it had never flooded.

I looked at my landlord and said, "It was God. We've been praying all day about this. My friends have been praying. This was God."

My landlord was trying to make sense of it all. He started to get an idea of what had happened and explained, "The last time that this happened, I installed these floors that were recommended by the water retention people. They're actually like this waterproof flooring." That was one of the reasons the water didn't get in.

He continued, "You know why else the water didn't get in? Because your friends came within an hour and water vacuumed all this water out. Toni, I don't think you understand. The water was flowing out of your house down the hill that you live on. It was a ton of water. This is unheard of."

"No, this is God," I said.

Lean in. This is God's miraculous power working through community. And this is why we don't heal alone. Because my friends literally came to rescue my home. The God who did it for me loves *you*. He wants to rescue you. He wants to get you to the place where you have enough capacity to know that the pain won't crush you. He wants you to have moxie, grit, resilience, faith, belief that no matter how dark it gets, light is there. Hope is coming. It's pumping through your veins. Even right now as you hear this story, you're becoming more hopeful. Your brain is starting to rewire and believe that He and His people are coming to rescue you. You can say:

"Oh wait, the pain is not wasted."

"Oh wait. I will actually make it through."

"Oh wait. I will not drown."

"Oh wait, I will not be crushed."

"And if I feel crushed, and if I feel brokenhearted, God's coming for me because He says in His Word that He's coming for the weary."

Are you weary? He will give you rest. Are you brokenhearted? He will be close. Do you need people to show up for you? He will send them. And they will be the right people for the right place and the right time. How do I know? I've witnessed it, I've seen it in my own life. And let me toot my own horn as I think about the bomb team that I have built over the past three years, who have helped me overcome some of my darkest days. I've needed them. And you need your own too. We all need friends who

- **Share their resources.** They may not be in the same state or country, but they can help us find a new house or resource or job. Their doors are open as they pray for us and find a way to help us from miles away.
- **Aren't afraid to get in the trenches.** They're nine miles away and don't mind getting their hands dirty to make sure that we have a safe home. They'll offer to take out our trash, and as single moms it will make us cry every time.
- **Have a similar story of pain.** These besties will witness our pain because they've been through it too. They're consistent and nonjudgmental. They text us scriptures every single day when we can't find the words to pray.
- **Are justice driven.** They will fight for what is just in our

lives and righteously call out the person who hurt us most. They will remind us that we're worth more than the pain we've been through and tell us that *God knows* and hasn't forgotten us.

- **Call us "queen" when we least feel like one.** They will give us confidence when insecurity tries to rear its ugly head.
- **Are prayer warriors.** They will slay Satan with their words that glorify God and give practical advice in the weary moments. These friends will ask us to turn on our spiritual ears and hear the voice of God.
- **Are ready for a good time.** A fun encourager will randomly call us, even though nearly our entire generation hates phone calls. They'll talk with us on our rides just to check in and hear our voice. They may also book a massage to help us relieve the stress of healing.
- **Keep us accountable.** They will hold us to the integrity we desire and text us to check in on those things we use to numb or hide. They pull us back into the never-linear, never-easy healing journey with integrity and grace.
- **Make us laugh.** They will send us the most encouraging texts—coupled with ten dollars for a latte—and some of the funniest memes and videos on Instagram.

You need to build your team. And I say that in the kindest, most encouraging way that I can. Because I know what it's like to do this life alone, I know what it's like to heal alone. And listen, doing it with others is the only way!

One last thing I want to leave you with about this. In 1 Corinthians 12 the apostle Paul spoke about the body as a team with different roles. "Just as a body, though one, has many parts, but all its many parts form one body, so it is with Christ. For we were all baptized by one Spirit so as to form one body—whether Jews or Gentiles, slave or free—and we were all given the one Spirit to drink. Even so the body is not made up of one part but of many" (vv. 12–14). Paul was referring to all of the spiritual gifts in believers and how, while they may show up differently in each of us, they all still have one common purpose and goal. The body of Christ could not work as it was intended if every part were the same. If we were all hands or all feet, we wouldn't be the complete body.

If humanity is God's plan A for redemption in this world and He made us all with unique external and internal giftings to build His church and saturate the world with goodness, He also had a plan for how this would play out in your healing journey. Come on, open up those spiritual eyes and look at what God has for you! He's not just interested in building His kingdom with people; He wants to build His kingdom with healthy people who are pursuing wholeness. God knows that the best version of this world is a world saturated with people who haven't let trauma, insecurity, pride, anger, fear, pain, and doubt have the final say in their lives. And let me tell you what those people have in common: They don't do this life alone. They are intentionally connected to the rest of the body. They know they can't do it alone and that all parts are needed to not only survive but thrive. I believe God wants His people to thrive.

Think on This

Let's reflect and dive deep for a moment. What part of your team still needs building? Are you missing a metaphorical hand? A leg? (That got weird!)

Read the following descriptions of types of friends. Then fill in the blanks after the reflection questions with the type(s) of friends that you need.

The Deeply Connected Friend: This person has experienced similar pain and can deeply relate and provide wisdom.
The Spiritual Guide: This friend really challenges you in your faith and your relationship with Jesus.
The Healing Accountability: This one talks to and encourages you in your counseling or healing journey.
The Cheerleader: This person will send you an encouraging text out of nowhere, show up on the sidelines of your life, and push you toward hope.
The Challenger: This friend is the one that you need to help lead you to righteous conviction, hold you accountable through your temptations, and lovingly get you back on course.

Who are you missing in your life? _____
Who in your life are you expecting to play a role that they can't? _____
Who do you need to ask God to send your way? _____

Who do you need on this healing journey with whom you can practice withness? _____

Not only can we not do this healing journey alone, but we also can't do it without the right team in place. Not to worry, we've got the best head coach in our heavenly Father, and He knows. God knows just who to send. Trust Him to do it.

Chapter 10

EMBRACE DIVERSITY

Amanda and Payal's friendship will forever be seared in my brain as one of the most beautifully opposite relationships I have ever witnessed. Amanda is a White American woman and Payal is a Pakistani woman. Both women were at a Zumba class in Florida when something amazing happened. They tell the story better than me, so here goes:

From Payal: I am married with two children. I raise my kids in the same city where I grew up. A lot has happened in the last few years: 9/11, Afghanistan, the Iraq War, drone strikes, and sanctions, to name a few. Divisive political campaigns along these issues, spewing rhetoric that personally affected my family: immigration, the Muslim ban, and Islamophobic tropes. It was a hard time for my family.

I distinctly remember my youngest crying the day one

of the elections was called because she was afraid that "they are going to kick us out." Then I randomly met a sweet, kind human named Amanda at a much-disliked Zumba class at our local gym. (I don't like exercise and I have no rhythm.) But our meeting was fate. Amanda approached me and told me that I was not alone, that she also struggled with the divisiveness in the United States. We started meeting for coffee and ultimately decided to host a gathering of her friends and my friends to share a meal and create a greater community outside our silos.

I also remember Amanda's peacemaking shirts, and I would always compliment her. She told me they were from an amazing nonprofit group that she followed, and that I should check them out. Peacemaking nonprofit? Whoa, what's that? That sounds pretty cool. I didn't even know that was a thing!

Not much later, the nonprofit she was a part of led a campaign for people who were "looking to heal divides in their community." Amanda asked me if she could contact them about our newly formed group. That's when I started really digging in. I looked at the website; I read the blogs; I fell in love and was sold. Soon after, Amanda and I both joined the team as frontline coordinators, a dream job where we encourage people to gather in their own communities to listen, understand, and grow in empathy for those different from themselves.

I have always been someone who desires peace, and the best part is that I am not alone. The more we work in community to do the hard work of peacebuilding, the more success we will see. It's also definitely more fun.

A few years after Amanda and Payal met, I joined the team[1] as the director of the frontline coordinators, and I got a chance to see up close what it looks like for two people from two different backgrounds to love each other well—in the face of their differences. This wasn't a front to promote peacemaking; they were truly friends, caring for each other, their families, and their children. They deeply knew each other. They didn't let differences make them put up walls or keep them in their silos. This was a close-up look at humanity choosing each other and connecting through pain. Working with and leading Amanda and Payal opened my eyes to be more inclusive in the way that I choose friends.

Embrace the Different

What could being more open to differences in people in your circle bring to your life? What could leaning into the unlikely and the unknown do for your heart? What's stopping you from embracing differences in your friendship circles? I think Jesus modeled this really well for us. When my daughter and I walked to our car hand in hand after church one day and I asked her what she learned in her service, she said that Jesus was her good friend. He's a friend to us all. Young, old, and different. You may have heard the following story from the Bible, but let's unpack it together with the lens of Jesus befriending someone in the face of difference.

One of the most powerful stories from the Bible where Jesus embraced someone whom society labeled as unworthy due to her difference and her story is the encounter of Jesus and the Samaritan woman at the well. This beautiful moment of compassion, recorded in John 4:1–42, highlights Jesus' radical approach to inclusion and compassion, challenging all kinds of societal norms and prejudices of His time. And it proves that embracing differences could be the very thing that radically changes someone's life.

Let's start with a little bit of context, because we need that! Scripture always needs context. In the cultural context of this time, Jews and Samaritans had a long history of mutual animosity. The Samaritans were seen by the Jews as ethnically and religiously impure because of their intermarriage with foreigners and their different religious practices. Additionally, the gender dynamics of the period dictated that men, especially rabbis like Jesus, did not engage in public conversations with women, particularly those who had a broken or sinful past and a bad reputation because of it.

As Jesus traveled from Judea to Galilee, He passed through Samaria and stopped at Jacob's well in the town of Sychar. He was tired from his journey, so He sat by the well around noon. A Samaritan woman came to get water, and Jesus initiated a conversation by asking her for a drink. This simple request for water broke several societal norms—like, all of them. Even the woman was surprised, and she questioned why a Jewish man would ask a Samaritan woman for a drink.

Jesus' request was not just a matter of quenching His thirst but a deliberate act to engage with the woman. He knew what He was doing! He knew what was on the other side of that encounter full of difference. He disregarded the ethnic hostility and the gender norms, treating her with dignity and respect. Jesus then offered her "living water," a metaphor for the eternal life and spiritual fulfillment that surrendering to Him brings us all. This offer intrigued the woman, leading to a deeper theological conversation. I love this. I love that a simple drink of water led to curiosity and deeper conversation! I believe that's where the good stuff comes from.

During their conversation, Jesus spoke about her personal life—that she had had five husbands and was currently living with a man who was not her husband. This part of the conversation was significant because it showed that Jesus was aware of her situation and still chose to engage with her without judgment. Instead, He modeled curiosity for her, and for us today. The woman recognized Jesus as a prophet and brought up the longstanding religious dispute between Jews and Samaritans regarding the proper place of worship.

"Sir," the woman said, "I can see that you are a prophet. Our ancestors worshiped on this mountain, but you Jews claim that the place where we must worship is in Jerusalem" (John 4:19–20).

Jesus responded by giving her a revelation around the future of the religious dispute, emphasizing that true worshipers will worship the Father in spirit and truth, regardless of geographical location. He then told her who He was—the Messiah, the Christ. His revealing Himself to her was a huge deal, given that she was a Samaritan and a woman with a broken past. This was one of the few instances in the Gospels when Jesus directly identified Himself as the Messiah, and of all people, He chose to do so with someone who was considered an outcast. I love moments like these in the Bible! They're like a little holy soap opera.

The Samaritan woman, deeply transformed by this encounter with Jesus, left her water jar and ran back to her town, urging the people to come and see Jesus, whom she believed to be the Messiah that had finally come. Her testimony led many Samaritans to believe in Jesus, and they invited Him to stay with them.

Wait, hold up—let's not hurry past this. Her encounter with the one true God, who didn't hold back because of her difference, her reputation, her exclusion, her doubt, led a whole group of people to follow Jesus, the one true healer of our hearts and souls. Because sometimes our yes to difference can impact an entire community. Just like Payal and Amanda.

Jesus stayed for two days, teaching and sharing His message, resulting in even more Samaritans coming to faith.

The story of Jesus and the Samaritan woman at the well highlights Jesus' mission to break down barriers and extend grace to those marginalized or too different for society to accept. His willingness to engage with the Samaritan woman demonstrated that His message of love, acceptance, and salvation was and is for all people, regardless of their ethnic background, gender, religion, or past sins. This story challenges all of us to embrace inclusivity and compassion, companionship and belonging, no matter what.

Tearing Down Your Own Walls

I remember the moment I realized that though I have always been an inclusive person, there was a wall up. I would befriend anyone and everyone, no matter what they looked like, but I would go deep only with people that looked like me. It wasn't until I was around twenty-five that I started opening up my heart to women who were Caucasian, Asian, Hispanic, and so many other ethnic backgrounds. It happened when I met Payal and Amanda.

I have to be honest about this. I didn't feel like I'd be able to connect deeply with someone of a different race—that was, until I met Eryn in a greenroom at Gwinnett Church and her story was so similar to mine that it blew my mind. She'd started an organization called So Worth Loving, helping people believe in their undeniable worthiness that was given to them at birth by Jesus and couldn't be taken away. (And the cutest merch you've ever seen!) She'd also gone through a hard divorce where it felt like the church she used to attend pushed her away.

The difference was, she was a bit further ahead in her healing journey than me—and wow, she changed me. She told me things about the healing journey I hadn't discovered yet after my first divorce and hopping back into ministry. She referred me to books and was even the one to introduce me to my sexual trauma counselor and betrayal group. My being open to difference helped me on my healing journey in ways that I just don't think I would've gotten if I hadn't been open to having a real friendship with someone who looks completely different from me. I'm Black, she's White. I have little tattoos; she's got a whole sleeve. My hair is dark brown, hers is bright blond. I'm average height, she's shorter. We dress differently, talk differently, and yet our stories divinely connect us. We have been doing life together for six years now. She has seen me through some of my darkest days, and I've done the same for her. I really don't believe I would be this far into my healing journey if it wasn't for Eryn.

Reasons to Embrace Difference

Being open to friendships with people who are different from us, I believe, is essential for our healing journey. Our diverse relationships can give us unique support, fresh perspectives, and opportunities for spiritual growth, and all of these things contribute to our well-being and healing process. If I haven't already convinced you to lean into this, here are eight reasons:

1. Difference can transform you.

In our healing journey, experiencing God's love through the kindness and support of others is transformative. Diverse friendships allow us to encounter God's love in various forms and expressions. When we form relationships with people from different backgrounds, we experience the multifaceted nature of God's love and grace. This can be incredibly healing, because it reassures us of our worth and helps us feel seen and valued in our unique circumstances. Just like Eryn did for me.

2. Healing often requires a shift in perspective.

Many of us need to go from hopeless to hopeful, believing that things can actually get better. Engaging with people who have different life experiences can provide new insights and wisdom that we might not run into within our familiar circles. These diverse perspectives can challenge us to think differently about our own struggles and offer new approaches to healing.

For example, someone from a different cultural background might have different coping mechanisms or practices that could be beneficial to us. In the African American community, counseling has been frowned upon for decades. Stepping outside of that part of my community and embracing counseling is one of the foundational reasons I'm still standing.

3. Embracing diversity brings more empathy and compassion.

Forming friendships with people who are different from us helps build empathy and compassion, both of which are crucial for our healing. When we understand and appreciate the struggles and joys of others, we become more compassionate toward ourselves. This type of empathy can soften our hearts and help us forgive ourselves and others, which is often a significant step in the healing process.

4. A diverse support system is robust and resilient.

When we surround ourselves with people from various backgrounds, we tap into a wide range of experiences, skills, and resources. Diversity can provide more comprehensive support during difficult times. Different friends might offer different types of support. Some might offer practical advice, while others provide emotional comfort or spiritual encouragement.

I remember when I moved myself, my kids, and our nanny into a new house after my second divorce. It was tough. Maybe the hardest thing I ever had to do was leave the home I thought I would grow old in. I decided to do a Christmas Eve potluck at my house and invite all my friends. The rules were simple: Wear pajamas and bring a cuisine representative of your culture. I gave a little speech and looked around the room at all the different faces I'd befriended along the way. I can still remember the smell of everyone's different cuisines filling my home with love, joy, and true welcome. It felt like what heaven would feel like one day.

5. We can learn from others' experiences.

Everyone has a unique path to healing, and by forming friendships with people who are different from us, we can learn from their experiences. Hearing about how other people have navigated their own challenges and found healing can inspire us and provide practical strategies for our own journey. These stories of resilience and recovery can offer hope and remind us that healing is possible, even in the face of significant pain.

6. We grow by stepping outside of our comfort zone.

Diverse friendships encourage personal growth, which is an essential component of healing. These relationships challenge us to step outside our comfort zones, confront our biases, and grow in understanding and maturity. This personal growth can lead to greater self-awareness and emotional resilience, both of which are important for healing. As we grow and change, we become better equipped to handle life's challenges and continue on our healing journey.

7. We live out the inclusive love of Christ.

Reflecting Christ's inclusive love to others can be a source of healing in itself. When we embrace diversity and form friendships with people who are different from us, we become more like Jesus and treat His people more like He would. This act of love can be healing for our own souls, because it aligns us with God's will and purpose. It also brings joy and fulfillment, knowing that we are contributing to a more inclusive and loving community. I smile every time I see my daughter realize how beautifully diverse our friend groups are. I can tell she notices by the way she has started to lean into friends of different backgrounds in her own life. I am contributing to the way she views her community by being intentional about the way I cultivate mine.

8. We move toward overcoming feelings of isolation and alienation.

Diverse friendships can foster a sense of belonging by showing us that we are part of a larger community. When we are welcomed and accepted by people from different backgrounds, we feel a sense of connectedness and solidarity. This feeling of belonging is crucial for emotional and psychological healing, as it reassures us that we are not alone in our journey no matter our background, our skin color, or age.

I hope this chapter has opened your eyes to the importance of difference in friendships on this messy, never-linear, sometimes painful healing journey. I know it's already hard to find friends, and adding in differences makes it especially challenging. But this is a peek into heaven, my friend. A place where our differences will reflect how big God is and how intricate He decided to be when He created all of us. This is what makes God, God. He is the central thread, tying together all of our uniqueness into a single, beautiful truth: We are not alone.

Different is good; it's real good. How do I know that? Because God is good. And if He decided to create us all with difference, He intended for it to be very, very good.

Stretch yourself outside of your comfort zone, talk to the person who puts you out of your comfort zone, join the neighborhood Zumba class and comment on the shirt someone's wearing that you've been eyeing, let the one woman into your small group that you don't think will fit in, and then carefully and prayerfully pull them in—closer and closer. Until one day you'll look up and realize that the Eryn or Amanda or Payal in your life changed you in ways you didn't expect. And you never

You could change an entire community by choosing to love and be loved as Jesus did: radically, wildly, beautifully, lovingly inclusive.

know—you could change an entire community by choosing to love and be loved as Jesus did: radically, wildly, beautifully, lovingly inclusive.

Think on This

- What are some unconscious biases or beliefs you have about those who are different from you?
- What are some ways you can widen your circle outside of what you're comfortable with?
- Which of the eight reasons did you most resonate with?

Chapter 11

CREATE YOUR OWN CONFESSIONAL COMMUNITY

I remember the night we gathered as a confessional community for our first retreat. We were in the hills of Texas tucked away at a retreat center that showcased the vastness of God's creation, and I felt so scared and awkward. We sat down in a living room surrounded by windows, trees, and fluttering hummingbirds that would hover in front of the windows as if to say, "Calm your fluttering hearts, God is near." And while maybe we knew that of course God was in the room, we were also deeply afraid of what it would mean to confess our sins in community. Because that's what the confessional community is. A secure place where no matter what doubts, fears, addictions, tensions, and hurts you bring to the table, nobody, and I mean nobody, will ever leave the room. Because Jesus never leaves the room.

One of the ladies in the group said, "We all get to be like Jesus with skin on for each other." Dr. Curt Thompson, the psychiatrist that we brought in, said, "We are practicing withness when we sit with each other in our pain. Withness is the currency in our community. And, while every confessional community doesn't need a professional counselor, if there are any people in the group with past trauma, it's definitely a tool that has helped us in ours."

My Confessional Community

After our first in-person retreat, we decided to have a three-hour Zoom call every month. We thought it would be good to have a monthly check-in with all seven of us, which gave us an adequate amount of time to be there for each other. Maybe that looks like one hour a week for your group. Or two hours biweekly. The goal is to help each other feel and become more seen, soothed, safe, and secure. We have a text group where we check in with each other weekly to share what we are going through, ask for prayers, and send encouraging words that become lifelines that help us get through our day-to-day struggles. (More on how to practically set up your confessional community at the end of this chapter!)

For our first retreat we flew in from Canada, Georgia, other parts of Texas, and Washington, DC. After we realized the depth of what we had signed up for, one person asked if we all needed to make a blood pact sacrifice, ensuring we were fully committed to confidentiality and safety. It was dramatic for sure. After all, for shame to leave the room, safety is needed. And with a past like mine, filled with trauma, I really did need a safe space to heal. To my surprise, so did the other women. Maybe all of us do. Maybe we all need a confessional community where people show up, confess what we have going on, and hold each other's pain and meet it with empathy, words of kindness, and prayer. And maybe we all need a friend or three or six to promise with everything in them that they will never breach the trust of the group.

It's very difficult to heal in the place or with the people that broke you in the first place. But it's quite the opposite when you keep showing up with people who have helped you heal, and it's only that much more special when you can return to familiar places with those people, like an annual retreat. When you sleep in the same rooms and look in the same mirrors and witness the growth, the redemption, the grief and pain, and how we don't have to hold them alone, the bond between you smells of redemption and creates a holy attachment. I think this is why God designed us to dwell together. The healing power of witness is something I'll never take for granted. My confessional community has healed parts of me that I didn't even know needed healing.

My confessional community has saved my life. And I know that the other women in the group would say the same. Jesus was clear when He said that we will have peace in Him and trouble in the world. He even said that we would need to take heart (John 16:33). I don't think He said any of this to scare us but to prepare us for the reality of the pain, tribulation, and hurt we would indeed walk through on this earth. The power of a confessional community is that you don't have to wade through those waters alone. When my friends and I realized the power of what this group meant to us, we wanted to tell the world about it! I even incorporated this as a next step for my women's course groups. And now I want to offer this to you as you are taking steps to walk away from healing alone and press into healing with others.

How to Create Your Own Confessional Community

I am asking you to lean in and consider something that feels vulnerable. Consider a community that isn't just about celebrating your kids' straight A's, your new promotion at work, a PR at the gym, or your spouse's promotion. Instead seek out a space where you can celebrate those and also talk about your deepest griefs. Maybe you've been so hurt by the people in your communities that you can't even fathom the thought of telling someone a dark secret of yours. I know, I know, this may make you sweat a little.

My friend Kristy found herself facing the sweat when she told her story bravely to one of her best friends. She stands on stages and tells the story of when she admitted to infidelity to a close friend, who then walked with her through the painful process of telling her husband. Unfortunately, her marriage ended in divorce, but there was her friend standing with her through the shame, and then holding her hand through counseling, healing, and rebuilding her life. Because that's what safe people do when you let them in.

Maybe the thought of showing up as your truest self is nauseating and feels so far from your reach. Or maybe you do have a community of people that you are meeting with weekly, like a small group from your church—but giving your opinion of a Bible study written by a well-known speaker or teacher is about as deep as y'all are willing to go. And maybe you're tired of meeting with people who know only half of the depths of you, and you long for someone to know the things that actually keep you up at night. Maybe it is time for you to invite the people around you more intentionally so that they can help hold the things that are crushing you. It may be time to share your burdens.

Wherever you are, I really do believe that you're reading this for a reason. There's a holy nudge here pushing you toward the light. Shame will tell you that hiding is better than stepping into the light. But as my counselor says, "Shame is like mold. It lives and grows in the dark, but it dies in the light." When you keep your secrets, your sin, in hiding in those deep corners of the dark, it will only produce more sin. Shame cannot live in the light, so step forward out of that corner and start pressing into the light that community brings. The goal for you and your group of people should be to be more like Jesus by the way you live and love those around you, including your own heart and body.

For my confessional community, my friend Jessica made personal phone calls to each one of us and talked through her idea of bringing us all together for a more intentional group friendship. I was in the airport when she called and started to explain how she had asked God to put women on her heart who would be a good fit. Some of the women said no due to time constraints or already being a part of a group, but for those of us that said yes, I'm so glad we did. Once all seven of us were locked in, it was go time!

Now, let's get practical and give you a peek into how we created and how we sustain our confessional community so you can begin to create your own.

Step 1: Choose your leader.

Jessica was our first leader. I remember that phone call in the airport. The whole time I was thinking, *Whew, this is a little weird, but I think I'm in!* One or two people have to rally the group, schedule the retreats and the calls, and not let up. The tension in these types of groups is vulnerability fatigue and fear. Sharing so much of your life so consistently can be exhausting, so having someone whose focus is to create consistency for the group will always be important.

Step 2: Schedule an in-person gathering.

I think we all learned during the global COVID-19 pandemic that being in the room matters. God made our good bodies to dwell with other good bodies. Pain is not something that can just be checked off a Zoom meeting agenda. Our pain needs to be held, gently rubbed, handed a tissue, and sometimes given a shoulder to lean on. Get in the room with people who

Our pain needs to be held, gently rubbed, handed a tissue, and sometimes given a shoulder to lean on.

can meet the needs of your pain. My group tries to meet in the same room once a year to give our pain a chance to be seen and known. It's important.

Step 3: Meet consistently.

Healing will cost you. It'll cost you money, time, and tears, it might make you anxious, and you'll definitely encounter grief. And it's worth it. You've got to be willing to invest your time into healing. Our group has decided that once a month for three hours is the consistency that we need. You won't always be able to be in the same room, especially if you're like us and live in different states. Figure out a consistent rhythm for your confessional community and stick to it. When vulnerability is met with consistency, it becomes a healing balm of connection and expectation. We expect our people to show up for us, because they actually do. Now, because we have had to go digital for these meetings, step 4 is very important.

Step 4: Ensure your meetings aren't hang sessions.

Be intentional here. We have a little time at the top of the call to do hang time, then we dive right on in. We typically have someone start our call off with a prayer, grounding exercise, or liturgy. Then one by one we express our griefs and longings in the moment. Our responses don't involve throwing out a scripture and moving on. We don't even attempt to fix each other's problems. Instead, we tell each other how we felt when they expressed their pain.

I know, I know, this is a backward view of what we have

been conditioned to believe that people need to heal. Don't they need that scripture to carry them? Don't they need that resource to get them to relief? Yes, of course. We all need the source that is our God to hold on to hope. And yes, we all need the resources that help us heal. But in this space and in this moment, what our bodies are longing for is withness. At this point you've heard that word ninety times. It's so important that we show up in ways for each other that drive us to connection. When we are in pain, we don't want correction; we want comfort. Be the comfort for someone in your life as they are the comfort for you.

Step 5: Repair ruptures.

This is a spicy one for those of us who don't enjoy conflict. But the truth is, when we are getting this intimate in our spaces with our people, there is bound to be conflict. We have had conflict happen right in the middle of our group when we're all together. We have coined it a "rupture." Well, ruptures always need repair. No matter what, if someone is offended or feels any negative emotion toward someone in the community, we always address it. Repairing ruptures creates safety. Hiding conflict creates false safety that can lead to bitterness and disconnection. Always, always, always repair ruptures.

I know this may feel intimidating and maybe even impossible for you. *Will anyone actually want to do this with me?* you may wonder. *Is it going to be awkward?* Spoiler alert: Yes, it will be at first. But it gets better.

Will I have time for this? These are such normal questions. My friend Jessica, who started our confessional community, says this: "We are each on a journey of revealing and healing the parts of us that simply need love and presence." When we let those afraid and lonely parts come into the presence of our friends who are hospitable to the parts of us we most hate, we get healed.

This sounds like a lot of emotional babble, but *it's actually real*! I am here to say: The vulnerability that scares you the most is worth it! We don't have to stay where we are. There is no part of you that is meant to be alone. There isn't one single part of your body, mind, or heart that is meant to do any of life alone. Down to our joints and blood and veins, we are an interconnected creation. And witness is our North Star.

Your Board of Directors

Here's the truth: Life is meant to be lived with others, and deep, lasting change requires deep relationships. You have to establish your "board of directors" (that's what I think of my confessional community as), the people who know every little crevice of you and love you just the same. The book of Proverbs is a book of wisdom that hits on a ton of areas of everyday life. Two of those areas are friendship and advisors. Multiple passages use the words "friend," "advisor," and "counsel." Remember that the Bible is an ancient book, so the idea of advisors or councils was very common for people living under a monarchy. Advisors and councils were often the subject matter experts of a given area of a kingdom. Today, even our government is set up to have a "council" of sorts to help govern the nation. Whether you're talking about a government council or *The Fellowship of the Ring*, the idea remains the same: A group of people all wanting the same goal can go further faster together. Or, in this case, heal further faster together.

I just want to say this: I am not talking about friends who are just going to tell you how cute you are and that God loves you all the time. Once I hit thirty, I realized I wanted some heavy hitters in my life to come in and shake things up. I needed some people who weren't afraid of holding me accountable or correcting me when I needed it the most. These are the types of people that you have to be able to depend on to tell you the truth when you don't want to hear it. Someone who is willing to show up even when they have their own life to hold. Someone who is committed to share the load of vulnerability by also being vulnerable themselves. People you can text when there's something hard in your life, and instead of texting back, they call because they know the power of being present and hearing the tone of where you are. You need friends who aren't afraid to stand in hard times with you and show up in their hard times too. It's more than just community, it's a community willing to confess and correct.

Proverbs 27:17 says, "As iron sharpens iron, so one person sharpens another." Let's talk about iron. The way a piece of iron is sharpened is by being struck. Sparks fly. Which doesn't really sound fun, does it? The striking movement is effective only when it's done continually and persistently. Over time the piece will go dull if there's no sharpening going on. So this scripture isn't talking about a one-time instance but a process over time. A process of refining and sculpting. And while at times it's not a fun process, it is a part of God's design to make us more holy. More like Him. God sent me these women who have been part of my life for the past three years. He sends us people, communities, villages to be His hands and feet so that we have help when we can't help ourselves.

In this passage, we see the importance of having wise people in our corner. People who are there for us, who want us to succeed and are a voice of reason when we lose our mind a little after a bad breakup, a terrible diagnosis, or a hard loss. A great council or board of directors doesn't just say yes to everything but will often disagree or push back on ideas. We all need a board of directors in our life. A group of people who want the best for us, want to see us succeed, know us, and know how to get the best out of us. These are people who will be by our side no matter what, and their opinions have a heavier weight because of built-up trust. These friends are willing to call out our nonsense, speak life into our hearts, and share wise words that point us in the right direction. Not only do we need these people, but we need to be that type of person to others. We need to be the type of person that seeks to make the world around us better and to be a voice of reason, love, hope, and truth.

We need our confessional communities. And guess what? They need us too. God's people are on the other side of your yes to leaning together into a life of healing, and the longings you have are the same ones they have too. So here's to confessing and connecting deeply. May we be so much better for it.

Think on This

Reflection time!

- What's the scariest part of creating a confessional community for you?
- Can you bring that fear to God and ask for His comfort?
- Do you have any people in mind who can be a part of your confessional community? Write their names down and begin to pray over what a conversation with them could look like.

Guess what? It's time for the third and final section of this book. You. Made. It! I'm proud of your willingness to press into deep, hard things. It's time to fill your backpack with some final tips and also hold up a mirror to who you want to be for others. Let's go!

Part 3

WHAT TO REMEMBER ON YOUR HEALING JOURNEY

Chapter 12

REMEMBER THAT GOD IS IN CONTROL

As I mentioned before, I get to lead a beautiful eight-week women's course where I help women heal and find hope again after heartache and trauma. It's an intentional, hard, and holy community of complete strangers who are willing to open up and say the hard thing so they can finally get freedom from shame and embrace that their brokenness isn't attached to their identity. In one of the hardest points of my divorce, I had a women's course scheduled. I began to pray about canceling it. I even asked my assistant, Amanda, to pray about it with me. I wanted to be able to show up fully as a leader for these women. I wanted to give them the best of me, and I was afraid that my own pain would stand in the way. We found peace that I should continue. Not because I wanted it to happen, not because my assistant thought it would be cool, but because God gave us peace about it. And by the end of the eight weeks, it was clear why God wanted me to do it. Reading the surveys still gives me the chills (or the holy tingle, as I like to call it):

Morgan: My year was hard and stressful but ending my year with this course gave me hope and joy in a way I didn't know that I needed. This course gave me deep friendships and a community of women who are safe and cared about what I said. I felt a sense of belonging and that was wonderful.

Jennifer: During my time in 100 Hopeful Women I have regained my hope. I have learned to focus on gratitude and prayer. This is the first course that I've completed and actually did the work to the best of my abilities. I miss our weekly meetings with Toni and the other ladies. Toni was so down to earth and open!

Sarah: God so intentionally put this course and these women in a season of my life I didn't know how much I would need them. Praising God for a biblically sound and safe community to rally around me in my pain.

Antoinetta: I didn't see the information about 100 Hopeful Women until the last day. Just that day I had prayed for more community, so I knew it was God. Healing is hard and messy and wonderful. Being in this group was absolutely wonderful and more than I could have ever imagined. Toni is brave and vulnerable, and it sets the tone for the group. It was a place of care, comfort and courage. These women are now sisters and friends.

There are a few things that I want you to know about these responses and these women.

First, I involved God in that decision because I knew that it is always by His divine hand and timing that His daughters get to experience healing and hope. This wasn't about what I was going through, this was about getting to create a space for women to discover and be who God already designed them to be. Women of goodness, of community, and of safety. We all shared our pain, and my choice to openly and vulnerably share my pain as I was facing it made God bigger. This wasn't about Toni the author or speaker; it was about Toni the broken daughter of God who needed Him and His people more than ever.

Second, these women and all the other women in the course agreed that being in a community was key while healing from really terrible things and circumstances. The word that has always and will always come up is "community." It was the key to their healing. Not the technology where we host the course, not the format of the calls, not the accessibility of the app, but the people. Your healing will always hit the ceiling that your community caps out at.

Third, these women were complete strangers. None of us knew each other. When we hopped onto our initial Zoom meeting, it felt like the first day at a new school. Everyone's eyes were wide open. We tried to make sure our lighting was great and our backgrounds were camera worthy. We didn't know what to expect from one another, but one thing divinely connected us: We were all desperate to heal and feel hopeful again. We didn't care what we did for work or what state or country we lived in. Our pain was what mattered in that space, not our positions.

Our desperation tethered us to the same valley that we needed each other to claw our way out of.

Finally, the women all mention the word "safe." I don't love this word when it comes to creating community. I feel like it's been abused and tossed around. I do not call what we do "creating a safe space," because the safety needed in healing cannot be found in building materials or video-call technology (I'm not a tech girly, so I have no idea what any of that is called). Instead, safe spaces are created with safe people. We are the ones who have to choose to be safe so we can help each other find safety. And the truth is, sometimes the people who are supposed to be the safest turn out not to be. Sometimes it's actually the strangers with shared pain who are the safest.

In a certain group I led, one of the women had a physical disability. She was stunning. Brilliant, kind, considerate, and so committed to her healing. A few weekly calls had passed before she really opened up—but when she did, we were all ready to go to war with and for her. She explained that over the past couple of years she had experienced medical issues that caused her to gain weight. As a result her mother had expressed not-so-kind things about her body.

We fumed. Some of us had motherhood wounds of our own, and we could feel the pain and damage that this behavior was causing our friend. Each one of us practiced withness, validation, and care toward her. We reminded her of her beauty. We rebuked the ways her mom had talked to her and put her down. We shared our own feelings that came up, and that day she walked away knowing that what she had experienced was wrong. I think she held her head a little higher as we ended the Zoom call. Sometimes the people who are supposed to be safe—like family—aren't.

More than anything, I was proud of her because she chose to bravely share something painful in front of complete strangers. She could've shut down and given up on people. She could've gone to one of the enemies of vulnerability—control. An unhealthy practice of control will short-circuit your healing process. Let me say this: Desire for control is natural. It gives us a feeling of stability and can bring safety to our hearts and minds. But if we put our desire for control in the driver's seat of our lives, if we lead with it, we could miss the opportunity to have a complete group of strangers become a community of fierce sisters fighting for us to feel seen and deeply known. When we fight for control, it causes us to put guards up out of fear that someone will hurt us. When we fight for control, we use only our logic instead of including our emotions in our relationships.

Can I tell you that one of the hardest things I've ever done was to give up control? To allow people in to help me during my most painful moments when I believed for so long that I could do better by myself for myself. I'm going to ask you what I asked myself: "What if God sent them?" What if God is trying to use His people to help you because they've got the strength that you don't have to make it through? What if God's attempt to work it all out for your good is through someone else's strength and not yours?

What if God's attempt to work it all out for your good is through someone else's strength and not yours?

First Kings chapter 8 talks about the idea of God using someone else's strength rather than that of the person who was originally supposed to do it.

> While the whole assembly of Israel was standing there, the king turned around and blessed them. Then he said: "Praise be to the Lord, the God of Israel, who with his own hand has fulfilled what he promised with his own mouth to my father David. For he said, 'Since the day I brought my people Israel out of Egypt, I have not chosen a city in any tribe of Israel to have a temple built so that my Name might be there, but I have chosen David to rule my people Israel.'
>
> "My father David had it in his heart to build a temple for the Name of the Lord, the God of Israel. But the Lord said to my father David, 'You did well to have it in your heart to build a temple for my Name. Nevertheless, you are not the one to build the temple, but your son, your own flesh and blood—he is the one who will build the temple for my Name.'
>
> "The Lord has kept the promise he made: I have succeeded David my father and now I sit on the throne of Israel, just as the Lord promised, and I have built the temple for the Name of the Lord, the God of Israel. I have provided a place there for the ark, in which is the covenant of the Lord that he made with our ancestors when he brought them out of Egypt." (vv. 14–21)

King Solomon, son of King David, ended up being the one to build the temple of God because David had blood on his hands.

We learn that King David had an affair with a woman named Bathsheba, who would become pregnant by him. When David realized this, he wanted to hide it. Hello, shame! He decided to hide it by doing the unthinkable—having Bathsheba's husband, Uriah, killed in battle. David was a warrior and had been through his fair share of pain, betrayal, hatred, and fear. Sometimes our choices can cause us to have to get out of the driver's seat and into the back seat, while we watch God's perfect plan play out.

This hits such a deep part of my story. When I went through my divorce, I lost so much at the hand of someone else's decisions to cause me pain. I lost bookings to speak, I lost the ability to put the book I'd been working on out into the world, and I lost control over my finances. And I didn't do anything wrong. I not only had to grieve a marriage that I thought would last until the end of my days, but I had to grieve not being able to stand on stages I believed God had for me to stand on and preach His Word. I watched conferences go on without me. I watched authors come out with their books when I was supposed to. I watched things be built while I was at home hiding from my children in the bathroom so that they wouldn't see my uncontrollable tears.

I know it feels unfair that the strength you need to keep going was taken from you, and now your grief is so heavy you can't even get out of bed. Small things that you once did without a thought, like answering emails, sweeping Cheerios off the floor, writing a short paper, and feeding and bathing yourself now feel like running a marathon.

REMEMBER THAT GOD IS IN CONTROL

Let me remind you that God's promises are always greater than our position in them. We should be "confident of this, that he who began a good work in you will carry it on to completion" (Philippians 1:6). This verse doesn't say that He will carry that good work through you; it says He will complete it. Sometimes that good work will be carried out through your people or the strangers that you meet who become your people.

My assistant, Amanda, became this person for me in the months when I took time away from social media and public platforms. I remember the day I decided to give her all my passwords and delete everything from my phone. I felt so inadequate. I was angry. *I am a leader. I speak to thousands all over the world. I have a podcast and am using my entire life to glorify God. I don't like people doing things for me that I can do for myself. And I can't answer emails? Am I being prideful? I just can't do it.* I couldn't believe it. I couldn't believe that the grief and the pain had become so fierce that I couldn't manage my own emails. And then God wrecked me—as He does. He reminded me that He didn't create me to do this life alone.

When sin entered the world, we came up against the curse of the enemy of our souls. Sin makes things suck. That's just the truth. And at the same time, Jesus makes things better. He has shown us the way because He Himself is the waymaker. He showed us what it's like to befriend the stranger and to offer aid, rescue, and redemption. I think about the moments people had with Jesus when they didn't know who He was. The woman at the well who felt like Jesus was straight-up trippin' when He asked her for water because of their belief differences. She had an encounter with Him that left her excited about the redemption His very life held. The woman who committed adultery and was about to be stoned to death found comfort and not conviction in the one true King of the world, having had no idea who she would be meeting that day in the temple courts.

These women had both experienced and committed discrimination, betrayal, adultery, shame, abandonment, and the fear of death. At their lowest point, a complete stranger, the Messiah Savior of the world, found them and gave them something that I believe He and His people can give you today—hope. Hope is the belief that things can get better. Are you ready to rise again? Just as Jesus Himself rose from death to life, I think He wants to bring some dead things to life for you too. It's time to hope again. It's time to allow Jesus to breathe life into your hopelessness.

It's time to believe in humanity again. It's time to trust again. It's time to bring your fears of trusting people from the grave to the operating room. Let God fix it. Let Him help you show up. It's time to be vulnerable again—or maybe for the first time. Get on the Zoom call, join the small group, go to that gym class and actually talk to someone, join that therapy group, or get on that app for people looking for friends. The people who hurt you don't get to have the rest of your story, okay? They've already done enough damage; they don't get to do more. If you submit your heart and pain to your loving Father, praying for Him to bring people into your life who can hold that pain, control won't get the final say. Healing will.

Think on This

Let's end this chapter with a liturgy. I have used a book of liturgies called *Every Moment Holy* in our course sessions, and it has provided beautiful reminders of who God is and what He is capable of when His people gather—especially strangers. This particular excerpt is from a liturgy called "Before Hosting." I pray that as you create space in your life to welcome in and host new relationships that could radically change your life, you remember these words:

> Grant to our company
> your traveling mercies
> in their comings and goings.
> May the swing of this door
> be to them as an invitation
> to shed their worries outside,
> and to enter here a space of rest
> and refreshment. But however
> they arrive, whether buoyant or
> burdened, may each know themselves
> welcomed and wanted here.

> Give us clarity and energy for the
> tending of details, but let us never
> prioritize logistics over love. Teach us
> always to unfold our "Martha arms"
> and open our "Mary hands." Let your
> grace be on display here. . . .
> May any who arrive as strangers,
> leave as friends. Let the simple gift
> of a seat at this table, and the experience
> of hospitable fellowship, long remain
> with our guests as a small reflection
> of your welcome, and as a reminder
> that with you there is no leaving.[1]

I am believing and praying these words and reality of welcome over you right now. Meet you in the next chapter.

Chapter 13

REMEMBER TO ASK YOUR COMMUNITY TO HELP CARRY YOUR BURDENS

You ever have an entire month that just sucked? Like every week, every day, every moment completely sucked. That was June 2024 for me. It was the first time in a long time that I felt hopeless. I mean, I'm a pretty hopeful gal. I see the glass half full, I enjoy forgiveness and redemption, and I really do believe the best in humanity. I'm usually a walking Teletubby! But that month I'd gotten really, really weary. Not necessarily my heart, or even my emotions, but my soul was weary. I felt like my spirit was being physically drained. And for a moment, I wanted to give up.

The first week of June we had our au pair company come

and film a weekend at our house to show what it is like to have a live-in nanny from Brazil help with children. I was so excited to show the world how special Anna Julia has been to me, especially as I walked through a divorce and created a brand-new life for my family. But on the first day of filming, our entire water system shut down. Six days before, I had finally been able to afford lawn care, and we were so proud of our little grass and bushes. Now they had to be dug up to replace the piping. I'm talking Blippi–style excavators and machines and men were all over the place as we tried to film. Unfortunately, they cut our internet wire while they were replacing the water lines, and our internet company had to come out and dig up another portion of our already ugly yard. It was terrible.

The second day of filming I got one of the worst migraines of my life and had to ask the film crew to change the schedule so I could take a nap. For an achiever like me, that was a hard one. But my vision was blurred, the pain in my head was blaring, and I was vomiting everywhere. And let's not forget that we didn't have water, so that was a pretty interesting moment when I peeled myself up from my toilet that wouldn't flush. TMI, I know. I'd never had a migraine like that and was so afraid that even a little bit of rest wouldn't cure it. The pain finally let up and we were able to film.

Once we got through the filming, I started feeling sick. I'd gotten a nasty sinus infection that was misdiagnosed as allergies, and the number of steroids and antibiotics I had to take for it for ten days was wild! Fortunately we had a family vacation coming up with my parents, my brother and his wife, and a few childhood friends in Texas. We'd been planning it since January, and everyone was so pumped about the beach house we had locked in.

We landed in Texas from Atlanta, got some lunch and a nap, drove two hours to the beach in the blazing heat, and once we got to our cutie purple beach house, we walked up to the door, only to discover that there were already people in the house. There were people already staying in our Airbnb that had been booked for almost six months. The despair that I felt at that point—wow. I got on the phone with Airbnb to find out that the owner of the beach house had sold it to a new owner, not told me, taken our money, and the new owners had already booked it out. Walking to our cars to tell my fifteen family members the news was crushing. Fortunately, we got into another Airbnb and connected with some friends that helped make our trip so much better.

Except, three days into the trip, I started feeling sick again and ended up in urgent care with strep throat. *I know, it's like it doesn't end.* We got home and I realized that it was my first Father's Day as a single mom. I'm not sure if it was the amount of medicine I was on, or just the real grief that I was raising a son on my own, but I cried all morning, I cried in church, and I cried as I pulled into my driveway—to a giant black snake staring at me. I know what you're thinking. *Was this a little garden snake, Toni?* No, it was not. It was a fully Crocodile Dundee wrap-around-your-neck big ol' black snake. Thankfully, I made it safely into my garage with the kids.

The day after Father's Day I opened my laptop and discovered the screen had gotten some water damage. I frantically moved this book's chapters over to Google Drive and thankfully was able to save it. One of the two horrific cherries on top was that I let Dylan, my daughter, go on a field trip to an amusement park with her class. Ten minutes after I drove away, her teacher called, frantic because they'd lost Dylan. For a whole hour, with the help of the police, we looked for her, and finally found her! But also, the amount of anxiety that washed over my body was next level. The second cherry was that finances were extremely tight since my speaking engagements slowed way down during the summer. For a traveling author and speaker like me, not being on the road speaking and selling books takes a real toll on my ability to provide for my family. I was sick, worried about finances, not eating, wrestling at night with terrible sleep, anxiety-ridden, and so weary. Down to my soul.

And then I remembered a scripture that I want to share with you again and encourage you to hide deep in your heart: "Carry each other's burdens, and in this way you will fulfill the law of Christ" (Galatians 6:2). Showing up for people is an act of biblical obedience. But this time, I didn't need a coffee date or a candle. I needed witness for my soul. For the first time in my life, I really did feel like I was in a spiritual battle. The enemy was coming for every single part of my life. My health, my finances, my heart, my safety. He was coming with everything he had. And if I'm honest, he was winning. I was so tired. Getting out of bed got harder and harder every day. I started to get scared that something horrible was right around the corner. I was afraid for my children, and at the same time I had little capacity to pray fervent prayers. I sat in my room and the only words I had were, "God, help me. Please. Help me."

When You're Weary

Maybe you've had one of those moments; maybe you're in one right now. You don't have the strength or the words or the hope to carry on. You're weary down to your soul. Your marriage isn't getting better. Your body is physically fighting to be healthy. You're afraid of when the next shoe will drop. You just can't see the end anymore and all you need is a glimmer to be hopeful again. But it's just not coming. Can I tell you what I did when I was there?

I was in Maine the last week of June on a video shoot for a show I get to be a part of called *Unshakable Moxie* with a ministry called Our Daily Bread. It had been a few days since anything crazy had happened, so my family and I were a little more stable. Then I got a text from Anna Julia saying that our electricity had shut down. She had to pack up the kids and take them to a friend's house. We were still being attacked, and it was the last straw for me. Before we left for filming for the day, I sat outside and sent this text to everyone I knew that would really do it:

> Hey y'all, I'm rallying the troops. I've been up against some really intense and persistent spiritual warfare these past three weeks and I'm so beyond weary. I've been fighting and praying with everything I have, and I just need some saints to

stand in the trenches with me. If you have the capacity, can you pray these things in agreement for the rest of the week until Sunday?

1. Protection for my nanny and kids while I'm gone for work.
2. Protection over my house. That no other maintenance or outages or snakes would bother us.
3. My strength and endurance. I have so much faith in God, I really do. I believe and can clearly see Him warring on my behalf. I'm just so weary.
4. Pray that my health stays good so I can show up for work and provide for my family.
5. That God would increase my finances swiftly so that my anxiety around money scarcity would be at ease and I can catch up and get out of debt.
6. That Anna Julia (my nanny) would be filled with joy. She's had a hard week, and I can tell that she's weary and scared about all of the things that keep happening to us.

Love y'all. Grateful for all of you. Believing for better days.

Sometimes prayer is the very thing your people can give you that makes all the difference. I believe in prayer with everything in me, and I enjoy praying, but I needed my people in the trenches for me this time. When I couldn't form the words, they did. When I couldn't get on my knees, they did. When I was afraid, I leaned on their faith. And maybe it's time you lean on the faith of your faithful few as well.

REMEMBER TO ASK YOUR COMMUNITY TO HELP CARRY YOUR BURDENS

Here's what I want to encourage you in: Be specific with your prayers! I needed to type out that text to my people because I knew if I asked them to pray, they would ask for what I needed prayer for exactly. They know that God is such an intentional Father to us that He wants every single detail. Philippians 4:6–7 says, "Do not be anxious about anything, but in every situation, by prayer and petition, with thanksgiving, present your requests to God. And the peace of God, which transcends all understanding, will guard your hearts and your minds in Christ Jesus." When the apostle Paul spoke into our anxiety, he was doing it in the context of a command, not a request. Paul wasn't saying that we wouldn't get anxious; he was saying that when we get anxious, we should remember that on the other side of our prayers, there's a miracle-working God who answers them according to His good and perfect will for our lives.

I also love that Paul used the word "every" in this scripture. Paul was teaching us that every prayer, every situation that we are wading through, is important to God. Everything should be prayed about. Looking for that promotion? Finances are tight and you're hoping for a random check in the mail? You've been on one too many dates that are awkward and you deeply desire for the next one to be normal? A loved one is not doing well, and you're believing for healing? Your big toe is hurting from wearing those heels a little too long that one night? Temptation from an addiction getting hard to manage? God wants it all. He doesn't leave one area of our lives untouched. He wants all of it to work for our good. So don't let shame win when you have

On the other side of our prayers, there's a miracle-working God who answers them according to His good and perfect will for our lives.

to rally the troops for prayer on your behalf. Lean in; give them every crevice.

I also want you to pay attention to the words "prayer and petition," or in other translations, "prayer and supplication." Prayer is a high-level idea, the act of communicating with God. Prayer is our conversation with Him, but petition is our direct asks of God. *I believe that the more specific we get with God about what we need, the more specific we will see His answers.*

What do you actually need, friend? Have you asked yourself that question? *What do I* actually *need?* Is it a companion, or the ability to find comfort in knowing that while you may feel lonely, you're never actually alone? Is it a new job, or is it a heart that is grateful for what God has already given you? Is it that you'd forget your ex, or is it that your heart wouldn't feel so heavy and you can sleep and eat again? Write those things down, get specific, and if you can't do it alone, ask a friend to help you write out your list. Sometimes our people know what we need better than we do. Tap into that.

The last part of this scripture I want to unpack for you is in verse 7, the promise of peace. This is what weary souls need—peace. This describes what we feel when we pray to God as the "peace of God." It surpasses anything we can comprehend. It doesn't make sense; it "transcends all understanding."

As humans we can't see the bigger picture past our pain, but God absolutely can. In His almighty power, He knows that it all ends good, so He has a peace that our earthly eyes just can't see. What's special about our relationship with God is that in our salvation we have access to His peace. We may not be able to understand it, but we absolutely get to tap into it. We get to experience the peace of God without even being able to fully understand it.

When July came, something shifted. I felt peace for the first time in a long time. I felt like something had lifted off of my home, my family, and my soul. I began to think about every single person that prayed for us and their responses when I first texted them:

Lysa: I'm praying right now, beautiful friend. God did not design the human heart to be broken. But when it is, He promises to be very close to us.

Brittany: Praying! I'm with you and proud of you! Also, sometimes the most spiritual thing you can do is take a nap. Our weary hearts, bodies, and minds need rest in battle. Love you, friend! Jesus sees, and He is more than able.

Kristen: Completely on it, interceding on your behalf and all of these petitions.

Rainey: *Heavenly Father, I pray in the name of Jesus that your hand of protection be over Toni, Dylan, and Sammie. We ask these things already knowing you are a God who sees and provides. You are Jireh.*

Amanda: Praying right now. Believing with you!

Jo: On it in prayer.

Lisa: On it, my sister. And thank you for being specific with these requests.

Marquise and Krystal: Praying with you by name daily, Toni. You are shouldering so much stuff. Weariness and weakness in this situation are normal. My heart just hurts over you having to shoulder so much. Grateful that you leaned on us spiritually. We got you.

These are the words of the righteous. These are the words of community. "The prayer of a righteous person is powerful and effective" (James 5:16). This is how you show up for your soul. You barely show up at all, actually. You tap into the people who show up on your behalf, and you let them cover you until you can cover yourself again.

Lean into this, please. The enemy will come after you with everything he's got. I know it—I've witnessed it. I've fought through it. And for the first time in a long time, I was so weary my hope was starting to fade. But I wouldn't dare let the enemy of our souls win this one. He doesn't get the final say. He is not on the winning team—we are. God is and always will be the winner! Daughter of God, hold on tight. Do not give in to the enemy's ways. He is only distracting you from real healing and hope. He doesn't want your soul to be well, so he's going to do everything he can to break you in every possible way. In your finances, your health, your relationships, and your deepest fears. Do not shoulder that alone; rally the troops.

Think on This

Let's practice what that looks like right now by filling in the blanks on a sample text that you can send to a friend who you know will pray for you!

Hey _____,

I am feeling weary, and I need some help praying over a few specific things. Can you pray these things with and for me?

I need prayer against _____.

I want _____.

I am afraid of _____, and I don't want to be anymore.

I need help with _____.

I am still hopeful about _____.

Feel free to use this template, create one on your own, or even edit this one a little. I want to encourage you to practice leaning in on your people and watching God work through the righteous sons and daughters in your life.

He knows you're weary, and He knows which prayers are assigned to you even when they come from someone else. Because He cares and He knows. He has not left you; He is not ashamed or upset that you are weary. In fact, He is closer to you now than ever before because He specializes in rescuing the lost, weary ones. He is close to the brokenhearted ones (Psalm 34:18). He will give you rest—He promises.

So let Him. And let them. The people that love you care for you. Your decision to send that prayer request text, email, or DM is an act of bravery and an act of war as the enemy of your soul tries to take you out! And if it's war the devil wants, it's war he is going to get. March on, friend, march on! You're going to make it. I promise.

Chapter 14

REMEMBER THAT GOD CAN USE STRANGERS

I was twenty-four years old when I realized that I was a *fan* and not a *follower* of God.

I got saved when I was twenty-one and started volunteering at a student ministry about a year later. I went from student volunteer to student leader, to student volunteer leader, to student director. I ended up getting hired on staff at the church I was volunteering at. It was a real big shift from the life I'd been living before I joined the church at twenty-one. I had been twerking, smoking, drinking, popping—all the things. It felt like whiplash when I got saved and suddenly I was leading a student ministry. It was a quick turn. So quick that I realized I was in ministry and being *performative* more than surrendered to God. I was standing up on stages, preaching to youth and telling my story, being honest and vulnerable, learning how to be a good leader. But on the weekends, I was out partying and drinking and, sometimes, getting high. I was living this double life because I thought that I could say yes to Jesus and not actually live like it. I also wasn't actively healing the areas of my life that I needed to and instead decided to show up and pretend on stage and numb in the shadows. And unfortunately, I didn't have a strong, God-fearing, honest community of people around me to hold me accountable.

It wasn't until I put community in place that my people helped me realize this wasn't at all the way I should've been living. Because that's what God-fearing people in your life do—help you realize things that you don't realize for yourself.

But I had work to do too. I had to personally pursue my own healing—and that started with matching my private life with my public life. When I went through my first divorce, I really wanted a deeper connection with God. I stopped cursing, I stopped smoking, I stopped drinking. I wanted to get rid of anything that stood in the way of my relationship with God. I really started to pursue Him and consistently meet with Him during quiet time.

Then I started going to North Point Community Church under the leadership of Andy Stanley. I met this phenomenal couple, Chad and Emily Johnson. Emily was a life coach for the Tom Patterson Institute, a coaching program that helps you figure out "What's my life about? What's my purpose? How do I do this life really well?" She agreed to take me through a three-day life-coaching intensive to help me map out my life.

During the life-planning sessions, she told me about an organization called Feminine Hearts Alive that offered a spiritual encounter.

She said, "Hey, I think you really need to go to this spiritual encounter if you're trying to hear the voice of God. To really know Him, you're gonna need to do some work." It was like a four-day camp for women. We would stay at a beautiful retreat center with sessions where we were challenged to go deeper with God. I was ready and excited to start living the life that I really wanted with Jesus.

At this point, I was living in a condo at the Battery, formerly the Atlanta Braves baseball stadium, giving tours of its apartment community and helping with events that cultivated community engagement. One day, a week before the spiritual encounter, I gave a woman named Elsina a tour for an event she was planning, and at the end of the tour, as I was walking her to her car in the garage, she announced, "I want to share a word of prophecy with you if that's okay. There are some things that I feel the Lord has put on my heart for you."

I was down for the cause. I turned my phone's recording feature on so fast. I was in a place where I really wanted to hear from God—was desperate to hear from Him.

"Yes, please," I affirmed. "Speak. Tell me what the Lord is saying, because I'm in a season right now where I'm hungry for Him."

And she began to tell me things that no one who didn't already know me should know. I had just met this woman. She talked about my daughter. She talked about redemption and

God using her, and it was really crazy. Then she invited me to her church.

"There's a healing and prophetic service," she explained.

And even as I was saying, "Count me in," I realized that I didn't even know what "healing and prophetic service" meant.

So I went to this service, and at the time it seemed a little weird. And while I understand it now, at the time it felt awkward. I mean, they had people dancing around in the church with flags. They were speaking in tongues. I didn't know what was happening. I sat all the way in the nosebleed seats thinking, *Y'all suckers ain't about to get me. I'm not going to get sucked into the weird side of church. I'm just trying to hear from God.*

After some praise and worship a lady got up and announced, "Hey, guys, we're going to do something special. We're going to partner up and prophesy to each other."

Say what now?

I thought, *Y'all can't just throw us out there in the deep end. Who? What y'all talking about? I don't even know how to spell "prophesy." Is it with an* f? *Is it a* ph?

I was really freaking out!

Then an older Black man, who I found out was Deacon Robert, came up to me and said, "You first, ladies first."

Really? Chivalry? I didn't want it right then.

So I essentially just lied to the man. Or, at best, took a guess at what God might say to him. "I feel like God is, like, so proud of you, bro. And He loves you a lot, like, a lot."

He just stood there. And he was dead serious—which is really unfortunate, because he thought I was telling the truth.

And maybe I was. I don't even know, because I didn't know what was happening.

Thankfully, he replied, "Thank you so much, sister."

Now it was his turn. "I'm just feeling from the Lord that you should read the psalm of your birth year, Psalm 91."

And I thought, *You're a stalker. How do you know that I was born in 1991? Who are you, psychopath?*

But when I got home after church, I found my Bible. (Yeah, I had to search for it.) I literally blew the dust off that thang, opened it up, and read Psalm 91. Well, don't hold your breath, because it did not do anything to me. It was just talking about lions and stuff.

Fast-forward a couple of days. I'm at the spiritual encounter. And I loved it. It was intimate, less than a hundred women in attendance. They used the book *Captivating* by John and Stasi Eldredge, and it spoke to me deeply about my femininity and how God sees me as a woman and how I am uniquely made in His image. The whole time I felt lavished on and loved.

And then we get to the point of the weekend where they sent us out to spend two hours of complete silence with God. *What? Silence?* I freaked out. I'm a raging extrovert.

I wanted to talk, and I wanted to frolic with my friends, especially my new friends. Well, I couldn't. I quite literally had to sit and be with God. They gave us prompts to ask Him, such as, "God, what do You think of me?" The prompt for this first session with God was, "Lord, what's my biggest lie? What's the thing that the enemy uses to lie to me about You so that I'm not close to You?"

I went outside and found my little spot under a tree. I had my black leather journal with a gold picture of Africa on it. I sat there and asked, "Lord, what's my lie?"

I didn't hear anything. You want to know what I was thinking about? If I tell you the truth, don't cancel me, okay? I was thinking about Instagram and celebrities and if any of my follows had posted anything fun. That's what came to my mind. *I wonder what they're doing . . . I wonder what's going on in their lives.* Then I started thinking, *What am I gonna eat? Is the chicken gonna be dry here at WinShape?* All these random thoughts.

Suddenly I heard the Lord repeating in my soul: "You're unsafe. You're unsafe. No one's ever protected you."

You may know my story. When I was just seven years old, I was exposed to porn. When I was eight I was sexually fondled by a family member. When I was thirteen, I was sexually manipulated by a much older guy. He came over to my house and took my virginity in my SpongeBob SquarePants bedroom while his best friend sat in the living room. And my relationship with men in general was very toxic and based on a place of deep pain and insecurity. There is a lot of pain in my story. And I'd always had this belief that if God were good, none of those things would have happened to me. I believed God had never protected me. I'd never been safe. Where were the adults? Why didn't they help me? Why didn't anyone come for me? Why did they allow darkness to enter into my story when I was so little?

Those are the questions you ask when you're alone, and they should also be the ones you allow others to help you answer.

When I asked the Lord, it was *that*: I'd never been protected.

Then we all went back into the sanctuary and were given whiteboards. The leader instructed, "Come up front, take a dry-erase marker, and write out your lie on the whiteboards at the altar."

I wrote mine out: *I am unsafe. I am unprotected.*

Honestly, it was freeing to know what I believed about myself, my life, and God. It wasn't just that I was promiscuous and wild and addicted and crazy and an alcoholic. I began to see that there was something greater at war with my soul. I was using all of these substances to numb. Alcohol and partying and weed worked for me, like an employee. They served me. When I didn't want to feel the pain anymore, I chose to hire substances to numb. I was outsourcing my connection with God.

Later we had another session about being silent with God. I returned to my spot and looked at a second card they'd given us with this prompt: "Close your eyes and ask the Lord to give you an image of how He views you."

I've still got it written down in that little Africa journal. (It's so helpful to go back and look at what God has done!)

Closing my eyes, I saw myself in the middle of a field with a long dress on. My head was all the way back looking up to the sky, my arms were open, and I was just spinning. I'll say that that is the most authentic version of myself being free in God's creation. I wrote that down in my journal.

I closed my eyes again and asked, "God, is there anything else You want to show me?"

I saw myself again in that field. Then I saw a lion coming after me. It was running toward me, but it wasn't getting closer. Which is weird, right? So I wrote that down in my journal too. I even drew the lion in the journal, because I wanted to make sure I had proof that I wasn't tripping and losing my mind.

The retreat ended and I headed home with a journal full of God moments and intimate relationships. It changed my life.

When I got home, I was super hungry for God. The retreat leaders encouraged us to keep talking to God, to keep asking honest questions, and to try to wait and hear from the Lord as consistently as we could. In our quiet-time prompts they'd given us, we were supposed to ask God, "What scripture would You have me read today?"

One day I was sitting on my fake black leather couch from Ikea having quiet time with God, and I asked, "What scripture would You have me read today?" I got this strong impression on my heart to read Psalm 91. And I thought, *No, Deacon Robert already got that wrong. I've already read that one.*

I asked again: "Lord, what scripture would You have me read today?"

Psalm 91.

So I opened up my Bible. There was no dust on it this time. And I started reading Psalm 91 from The Message translation.

> You who sit down in the High God's presence,
>   spend the night in Shaddai's shadow,
> Say this, "God, you're my refuge.
>   I trust in you and I'm safe!"

When I got to the word "safe," I started weeping.

Here was the lie, the very thing that the enemy had used to place a wedge between me and God: *I have not been safe. I have not been protected. If God was good, He would have come for me. He would not have let those bad things happen to me.* Suddenly God was leading me to His Word, to assure me that I had always been safe.

> He rescues you from hidden traps,
>   shields you from deadly hazards.
> His huge outstretched arms protect you—
>   under them you're perfectly safe;
>   his arms fend off all harm.

Did you catch the word "protect"?

> Fear nothing—not wild wolves in the night,
>   not flying arrows in the day,
> Not disease that prowls through the darkness,
>   not disaster that erupts at high noon.
> Even though others succumb all around,
>   drop like flies right and left,
>   no harm will even graze you.
> You'll stand untouched, watch it all from a distance,
>   watch the wicked turn into corpses.
> Yes, because GOD's your refuge,
>   the High God your very own home,
> Evil can't get close to you,

harm can't get through the door.
He ordered his angels
   to guard you wherever you go.
If you stumble, they'll catch you.
   Their job is to keep you from falling.
You'll walk unharmed among lions and snakes.

Y'all, if God ain't specific, I don't know who is.

You'll walk unharmed among lions and snakes,
   and kick young lions and serpents from the path.
"If you'll hold on to me for dear life," says God, "I'll get you out of any trouble. I'll give you the best of care if you'll only get to know and trust me. Call me and I'll answer, be at your side in bad times; I'll rescue you, then throw you a party."

Throw *me* a party? Yup. That's my favorite part.

Maybe you're wondering why Psalm 91 didn't mean anything to me the first time I read it. If that's you, I'll name it: because I didn't have eyes to see and ears to hear (Matthew 13:16–17). I wasn't seeing what God was doing, because I didn't want to see it. I was drowning in my pain and needed rescue. When I started to allow people into my life who pointed me to the light, the darkness started to fade. When I longed for God to show up, I saw that He had always been showing up. He had always been protecting me.

Okay wait. Maybe you're thinking, *Where was God when you were being exposed to pornography? And touched*

When I started to allow people into my life who pointed me to the light, the darkness started to fade.

inappropriately? And sexually groomed? How was God in those? It's easier to blame God for the pain in our lives than the actual pain causers. It's easier to blame Him than the darkness and the people that caused the pain. Because if we identify that the pain came at the hand of someone we're in relationship with, we'll be in more pain when we have to confront them, place a boundary on them, or remove ourselves from them.

Sometimes as a victim, it's really hard to leave. Sometimes we forget that God's original design was goodness for us; it was Eden. And the enemy of our souls came into that plan that was full of light and leaked darkness into it. Sometimes we forget that it was the God of the universe and all of creation that rescued us from darkness by sacrificing His Son. His only goal is for good to saturate the lives of His people.

God got me out of that toxic relationship at age thirteen.

God taught me self-control when it comes to my sexuality.

God reminded me that forgiveness is a choice of the brave.

God changed my entire life by giving me community.

God was there weeping with me.

God wasn't the perpetrator; He was the rescuer. And when I realized that, when my eyes were open to the truth, everything changed.

Now, I want to catch you up on the most recent season of my life. I got remarried during this season of learning who God was. And I really thought that my redemption story had begun. After finding out devastating news around betrayal with my now second ex-husband, I was in a season of deep pain, grief, and healing with my community. It was probably one of the hardest seasons of healing I've ever gone through. And nearly six years after my encounter with God and Psalm 91, I started getting encouraging texts from friends. You ready for this?

I got this sweet text from Ann Voskamp just before bed one night:

> Hey T, as I'm praying here, as I turn the lights out, I'm praying these specific words of Scripture for you, for Sammie and Dylan, for your brave beautiful heart.

The scripture that she sends me is Psalm 91. (So yeah, I'm weeping.)

Then Kristy Starling from Victory Church in Oklahoma City texted:

> I can't imagine everything you're going through, sis. I'm just asking Jesus to be so close to you. He is surrounding you on literally every side. He is your hiding place and your refuge. I was praying for you the other day as I listened to Psalm 91 by Anna Golden. "I know your faith is not wavering," she said, "but I also know you feel real pain and real heartbreak and real grief." Just want you to know you're covered, even if you don't see it or feel it.

Irene Rollins, an incredible Bible teacher and friend, DM'd this on Instagram:

Hey lady, seriously praying for angels to surround you. Praying Psalm 91 over you. Sending hugs and love your way. You're not alone. You are loved. You are prayed for.

And my friend Channing sent this:

This is the time when the Lord is establishing order, and with order comes the need to bring what ain't working properly to the light. I've been feeling this strongly as well. So I'm definitely praying for him with you.

The same God who protected and preserved you and Dylan as you were beginning your journey to where you are today is the same God who will protect you and preserve you where you are and for where you're going. Psalm 91 has your name on it. Go forth in truth and boldness. God is with and for you.

Look at God moving, right?

Not long after this, I was at a women's shelter that I get to volunteer at here in Atlanta. The room that I teach in, where I meet with my girls, had gotten a little facelift. They put some plants in there and some cute little stuff, and it was just so sweet. They had also put paintings with scriptures on the wall. One of my girls who I love so very much always sits in the front row and helps me out with teaching and praying and all the things.

At the very end, after I had shared some hard things about my story, she came up to me and gave me a big old hug. We were just squeezing each other and crying because both of us were heartbroken for all that we've been through. As I was hugging her and looking over her shoulder, I saw on the wall in the back of the room: *Those who live in the shelter of the Most High will find rest in the shadow of the Almighty. Psalm 91:1.*

Crazy, right?

Daughter of God, here's some good news for you and for me: God's still speaking through His Word. The words in our Bible are still speaking today. You want to know the character of God? You want to get to know His voice? Read His Word. Because in the depths of our pain and our despair, we need a North Star. We need truth. We need rescue. And we have a God who rescues. He's the best at it. And guess what? He wants to rescue you. Sometimes when we don't believe that for ourselves, we need other people to remind us. During my first divorce I was so scared to trust community and, honestly, I didn't have many people in my life pointing me to Jesus. It's still wild to me how after I started really pursuing the Lord, He not only met me but He sent His people to carry me the rest of the way.

Did you catch that in the story?

It was Emily who helped me map out my life and brought me to the spiritual encounter.

It was Elsina who spoke a prophecy over my life that led me to understand that God will speak through other people to get to you.

It was Deacon Robert who led me to more of my life verses in Psalm 91.

It was Ann, Kristy, Irene, and Channing whom God used to bring Psalm 91 back into my life all those years later.

And this is why even after people have hurt us or responded to our pain in wrong ways, we still need people. I know, I know. When you've been hurt by people, you don't want to trust people. My hope is that in sharing my story, I will help you understand that we don't heal alone, and there is still so much goodness in humanity.

Think on This

There are zero coincidences. Zero, none, nada. God is the master chess player, and He wants to show you how holy and aware He is of your story, your griefs, and your longings. He is undoubtedly coming after you in the smallest and biggest ways. It's up to you to see with eyes that are expectant and believe with a heart full of faith. It's time to remember that there's an enemy of your soul at the ready to destroy your connection with a God who wants nothing more than a relationship with you. Fight back. Use prayer. Lean on your people when you're weak. And believe He's on the way—because it's true. It's so true.

Chapter 15

REMEMBER TO BE A GOOD FRIEND WHEN SOMEONE ELSE IS IN PAIN

Well, here's our last chapter together, and I'm so hopeful about what it will mean for you to not heal alone, to decide that life is better connected and witness is but one brave step away. In this chapter I want to share from a different perspective. I want you to imagine yourself being the person that helps someone heal. What will your presence mean to a woman who's in a valley and just needs the witness of a person like you until she finds the strength to climb out?

I've been the girl who needed presence in my valleys. And I want you to know how well my community has shown up for me in the hard, ugly, messy, ratchet parts of my life so you know

What will your presence mean to a woman who's in a valley and just needs the witness of a person like you until she finds the strength to climb out?

that presence matters. I want you to know how they helped me discover things about me that I did not know were true. Like how worthy I actually am of being treated with dignity, honesty, and respect.

When I look back through all of my hardest moments this past year, one of the things that was super consistent was how my community showed up. My people have been Jesus for me. And I needed them to be, because what I've learned over the years, as you now know, is that we simply cannot heal alone.

One of the very first stages I got back up on after my second divorce turned out to be one of the biggest stages I've ever been on in my life. I'm not someone who gets nervous about speaking. I'm confident that God will show up, because all of this is for His glory anyway, but there were these thoughts running through my head.

Will this audience be distracted because they know my story?

Are they going to be judging me?

Will my presence here hurt the organization that invited me?

About thirty minutes before I was scheduled to speak, two of the women from my confessional community, Melissa and Ann, came back to the greenroom to see me.

"I'm freaking out. I don't know what to do."

As Melissa began rubbing my shoulders, Ann calmly instructed, "Take a deep breath, Toni. Now breathe out."

As I began to settle, Melissa offered, "Why don't we verbally process. What are you afraid of?"

And in that moment, I realized that it wasn't at all about my gifts or the invitation to share openly. It was that I wasn't sure if I was good enough anymore. I wasn't sure if the pain that I had walked through discounted me from using my voice. And it's still crazy that I'm the girl who insists that broken crayons still color!

Here's what I know now, what I saw so clearly in that moment: The enemy doesn't have any new tricks. That uncreative deceiver was playing the same old tune, and something in me was falling for it. The reason I created Broken Crayons Still Color was because I knew what it felt like to feel disqualified and still used by God. I knew what this phrase meant down to my core.

"I'm too broken. I can't be used by God."

That's the soundtrack of the enemy in my ears, in my head, and in my heart.

And yet through these two friends, who know every crevice of my life, Jesus was saying, "I made you for this." They were the physical representation of Jesus being present with me in that greenroom. I heard His voice insisting, "I created you for this. Go get 'em, Toni!"

I got on stage and did what I was made to do.

This said, I legit felt like I was having a stroke. Seriously, I was freaking out inside from the moment I walked on stage to the moment I walked off. I almost blacked out! But when I stepped offstage, my mom and my daughter were right there cheering for me in the second row. There was something incredibly special about having three generations of my life present in that moment. This wasn't just for me; it was to show my mom that she helped me be resilient, and to model resilience for my daughter.

When the event concluded, women came up to me, insisting, "You set so many women free with what you said. I've never heard that said on this stage. Thank you, Toni, for being brave."

I assure you, it was not me. It was 110 percent the power and strength of God. My buckling knees gave that away real quick. And the God who gave me the strength to get on stage after processing through a panic attack with my people and then say words that touched so many women in the audience—He is the same God who still has purpose infused on the inside of you. Yeah, you. You can be someone's Melissa and Ann. You can be the very reason someone gets back up again, breathes through a panic attack, and chooses bravery. You.

I'll say this again and again: God does not play favorites. It's not us. It is God, and He is calling me, you, all of us to love His people well. I hope you've discovered that the people you admire, the people with platforms, the influencers and preachers and teachers, are just broken, fragile, imperfect human beings. And they don't have any more or less than you because they're any more or less loved by God. We are all doing the best we can, and there's a real big God and a little small us. There will be times when you need the care and witness that a friend brings, and many other times you will be the friend providing the care.

Why You Should Step Up

Being a good friend to someone on their healing journey is a profound way to live out the teachings of Jesus and demonstrate God's love. For women, this support can be especially crucial, as it fosters a sense of community, understanding, and strength during times of vulnerability.

Jesus' ministry was marked by His love and compassion for those who were hurting. Throughout the Gospels, we see Him reaching out to heal and comfort those in need. For example, He healed the woman with the issue of blood (Mark 5:25–34), showing her compassion and dignity when others shunned her. By being a good friend, you reflect this love and compassion, providing a tangible representation of Christ's presence in your friend's life. Your support can remind them of God's unfailing love and bring them comfort during their healing process. Here are several reasons I believe you should strive to be a good friend to someone on their healing journey:

1. Healing journeys involve emotional and spiritual challenges.

As a good friend, you can provide a listening ear, a shoulder to cry on, and a heart that understands. Offering your presence and empathy can make a significant difference, as it helps your friend feel seen and heard. In addition, praying for and with your friend can offer spiritual support, reminding them of God's sovereignty and the power of prayer in their healing journey.

Scriptures like Psalm 34:18—"The LORD is close to the brokenhearted and saves those who are crushed in spirit"—can be a source of comfort and hope as you become Jesus with skin on for your people.

2. Whether physical, emotional, or spiritual, healing takes time and perseverance.

You can encourage your friend to keep faith and not lose heart. Remind them of God's promises and faithfulness, encouraging them to trust in His timing and plan. Hebrews 10:23 says, "Let us hold unswervingly to the hope we profess, for he who promised is faithful." Your encouragement can help your friend stay hopeful and resilient, even when the journey seems long and challenging. My friend Matt Chandler once said, "Endurance is developed! The only way to develop endurance is to sit in resilience. And the only way to have resilience is to learn to suffer well." While that sucks to read, it's so very true. Maybe someone needs to hear from you that they can suffer well through their pain and develop endurance in the end.

3. Healing requires practical support.

This could mean helping with daily tasks, offering transportation to appointments, or providing meals. By offering practical help, you demonstrate Christ's love in action. Galatians 6:2 encourages us to "carry each other's burdens, and in this way you will fulfill the law of Christ." Practical support not only eases the burden on your friend but also shows her that she is not alone and that her community cares for her.

4. Having a strong support network is vital.

As women, we typically heal eye to eye. By showing up for someone, you contribute to a sense of community and belonging. Community can provide emotional, spiritual, and practical support, creating a safe space for your friend to heal. Acts 2:42–47 describes the early Christian community as one that devoted themselves to fellowship and sharing with those in need. I think it's time for us to go back to that model, where we give and share and show up for people in our communities. Because if we're all chasing after serving each other, no one will go without!

5. Healing requires self-care and rest.

We really like to wear our capes, but sometimes we have to take them off and let them be worn by someone who may have more strength than us. You can encourage your friend to take time for herself, reminding her that self-care is not selfish but necessary for healing. Jesus often withdrew to solitary places to pray and rest (Luke 5:16), setting an example of the importance of rest. Encourage your friend to find activities that bring her peace and joy, whether it's reading, walking, praying, or spending time in nature.

6. Laughter and joy can be powerful healing tools.

This is for sure my favorite thing ever. I love to laugh, and I really enjoy making my friends laugh too! Proverbs 17:22 says, "A cheerful heart is good medicine, but a crushed spirit dries up the bones." You can bring joy and light into your friend's life by sharing uplifting stories, watching a funny movie together, or just finding moments of humor in everyday life. Joyful interactions can provide a welcome break from the heaviness of the healing process and remind your friend that there are still moments of happiness and hope.

While support is crucial, it's also important to set healthy boundaries and offer accountability. This can help your friend maintain a balanced approach to her healing journey. Encourage her to set realistic goals and take things one step at a time. Offer accountability in areas where she might struggle, such as sticking to a new routine or attending therapy sessions. Ephesians 4:15 encourages us to speak the truth in love, and part of being a good friend is gently guiding our friends toward healthy habits and decisions. This is the way of Jesus. He was all grace, all truth, all the time. We get to be like Him in the ways that we hold our friends accountable to their healing process. Remember my friend Debra? She holds me accountable with love and grace when it comes to numbing my pain. It has helped me so much!

7. Healing is a gradual process with many small victories along the way.

Celebrate these milestones with your friend, no matter how small they may seem. Acknowledging progress can boost her morale and reinforce the positive steps she is taking. Whether it's completing a week of therapy, experiencing a day without pain, or feeling a sense of peace after prayer, these moments deserve recognition and celebration. Romans 12:15 encourages us to "rejoice with those who rejoice; mourn with those who mourn." Sharing in your friend's joys and sorrows strengthens your bond and supports her healing. Celebrate your people. We all feel good when we accomplish something; it's no different in our healing journey.

8. Trust God's plan for your friend's healing journey.

It can be challenging to see someone you care about in pain, but it's important to remember that God is in control and has a purpose for their suffering. *You get to be a friend, not a savior.* Encourage your friend to trust in God's wisdom and timing, even when it doesn't make sense. Jeremiah 29:11 reminds us of God's promise: "'For I know the plans I have for you,' declares the LORD, 'plans to prosper you and not to harm you, plans to give you hope and a future.'" Your faith and trust in God's plan can be a source of strength and encouragement for your friend.

Being a good Christian friend to someone on their healing journey is a powerful way to embody the love and compassion of Christ. Through emotional, spiritual, and practical support, you can help your people navigate the challenges of healing while cultivating a sense of community and hope. By reflecting Christ's love, encouraging perseverance, offering practical help, and celebrating progress, you provide a lifeline of support and strength. And you not only aid in their healing but also grow in your own faith and understanding of God's love and grace. You get to become more like Jesus! Supporting a friend through her healing journey is a sacred and holy responsibility and a profound expression of Christian friendship, love, and discipleship.

How to Be There for Your Friend

Now imagine us sitting here, sipping our coffee, and chatting about life and friendships. I want to tell you something that's been on my mind as I write this book, because I believe that there's so much potential in you. You can be an amazing friend, and I want to remind you of that today. Here's what you need to remember:

Just be yourself. The most genuine friendships are built on authenticity. You don't have to put on a facade or try to be someone you're not. The right people will love you for who you are, with all your quirks and unique qualities. When you're authentic, you attract friends who appreciate you for exactly who you are, and that's the foundation of a deep, lasting friendship.

Take time to listen. Listening is another powerful gift you can bring to your friendships. Sometimes we think we need to have all the answers or offer the perfect advice, but honestly, just being there to listen is often enough. When you listen with empathy, you show your friends that their feelings matter. You create a safe space by being a safe person, where they can share their thoughts and emotions without fear of judgment. That kind of presence is so valuable and can make a huge difference in someone's life.

Be kind and compassionate. Your kindness and compassion are like a warm hug to those around you. Little acts of kindness, like checking in on a friend, sending a thoughtful message, or even just smiling and saying, "I'm here for you," can go a long way. When you show compassion, especially during tough times, you provide comfort and support that can be incredibly healing. Your friends will feel truly cared for, and that's a beautiful thing.

Be dependable. You know, being reliable and trustworthy is another cornerstone of being a good friend. When you say you'll be there, show up. When you make a promise, keep it. Being dependable builds trust and shows that you're a steady presence in your friends' lives. They'll know they can count on you, and that reliability creates a strong, unbreakable bond.

Grab your pom-poms. Let's not forget the power of encouragement. Life can be tough, and we all need someone in our corner, cheering us on. I believe that you have a wonderful way of uplifting others, celebrating their achievements, and boosting their confidence. Sometimes just hearing "I believe in you" can make all the difference. Your support can inspire your friends to reach for their dreams and overcome their challenges.

Forgive freely. Now, conflicts and misunderstandings are bound to happen in any relationship. What matters is how we handle them. You can have a forgiving and understanding heart by understanding the way Christ forgives and understands you. When you approach conflicts with a willingness to listen and resolve issues, it shows your friends that your relationship with them is strong enough to weather the storm. Forgiveness doesn't mean ignoring hurt feelings but choosing to move forward with a deeper understanding.

Give them your time. Investing time in your friendships is also crucial. Life gets busy, but making time for your friends shows that you value and prioritize them. Whether it's a coffee date, a phone call, or even a quick text to check in, those moments of connection strengthen your bond. Friendships thrive on these investments, and the effort you put in will come back to you in wonderful ways.

Don't expect perfection. I want you to remember that being a good friend isn't about perfection. It's about being present, caring, and genuine. You have all these beautiful qualities within you. Trust in them and let them guide you. Your efforts to be a good friend will not only enrich the lives of those around you but also bring you immense joy and fulfillment. You have the power to make a profound difference in someone's life, just by being you.

Next time you doubt yourself, think about these things. You are capable of being an incredible friend, and your presence in someone's life is a true gift. Embrace it, nurture it, and let your friendships flourish. You've got this, and I'm here cheering you on every step of the way.

Think on This

- Show up for people the way you would want to be shown up for.
- Don't expect perfection; go after honesty and connection.
- We are imperfect people living in a broken world.
- Go where you are celebrated, not tolerated.
- Choose celebration over competition.

REMEMBER TO BE A GOOD FRIEND WHEN SOMEONE ELSE IS IN PAIN

> I'm forever proud of you, of us. For all that we have braved, for all that we have fought for. And we are still standing. Okay, time to finish!

CONCLUSION

As we come to the end of this journey together, I hope you feel inspired and empowered by the incredible strength and healing that friendship can bring into your life. The path to healing is rarely a solitary one; it is often the love and support of friends that illuminates our way and helps us find the courage to keep moving forward.

In sharing these stories and insights, my aim has been to remind you that you are never alone. Healing with friends is a beautiful and transformative experience, one that enriches not only your life but also the lives of those around you. It is a testament to the profound connections that bind us together, breaking through the challenges and pain that we will undoubtedly face on this earth.

I didn't want the year after my divorce to be as hard as it was. I didn't want to be in pain as much as I was. But can I be honest? I wouldn't trade it for the way I got to experience community. To experience God's people loving on me and my kids and our nanny the way they did showed me a bigger God—a loving God. If this is the way His people show up, it's because

He made them that way in His image! He is a God of withness. And He's sending His people. So as you continue on your healing journey, remember to embrace these five things:

1. Vulnerability

One of the most powerful aspects of healing with friends is the ability to embrace vulnerability. And while it's hard to be open about your pain, it's so worth it. It takes immense courage to open up about our struggles, fears, and wounds. However, when we allow ourselves to be vulnerable, we create space for deeper connections. True friends welcome this openness with compassion and understanding, offering a safe haven where we can express our true selves without fear of judgment. We all deeply want to be loved—especially in our pain. We just have to get brave enough to allow people to see the pain they get to help heal.

Vulnerability is not a sign of weakness; rather, it is a testament to our strength. By sharing our stories and being honest about our pain, we invite healing into our lives. Our friends become mirrors, reflecting our worth and reminding us of our resilience. In these moments of shared vulnerability, we find the seeds of our healing.

2. Presence

One of the greatest gifts you can give to your friends, and one that you can receive in return, is the gift of presence. Being fully present means showing up, not just physically but emotionally and mentally as well. It means listening with your heart, offering a shoulder to cry on, and celebrating the victories, no matter how small. Presence is about more than just being there during the good times. It's about standing by each other when the going gets tough, providing unwavering support through life's storms. When we are present for our friends, we help them feel seen and valued, reinforcing the bonds that make our friendships so healing. And they will do the same for us!

3. Encouragement

Healing is a journey that often requires encouragement and empowerment. Friends play a crucial role in this process by reminding us of our strengths and potential. They help us see possibilities where we might see obstacles and inspire us to take bold steps toward our healing. Encouragement can come in many forms—a kind word, a shared prayer, or a heartfelt pep talk. It is the unwavering belief in each other's ability to overcome challenges and emerge stronger. Through encouragement, we empower each other to face our fears, embrace change, and pursue our dreams. We can do this!

4. Prayer

For many, faith and prayer are integral parts of the healing journey. Friends who share our faith can provide spiritual support that is deeply comforting and reassuring. Praying together, sharing Scripture, and offering spiritual encouragement can reinforce our belief in a higher power guiding us through our struggles. Faith reminds us that we are never truly alone. It offers hope and perspective, helping us see beyond our immediate pain to the bigger picture. When friends come together in prayer and faith, they create a powerful support system that can uplift and sustain us through even the darkest times. Go to the throne with your people!

5. Growth

Ultimately, healing with friends is about growth and transformation. As we navigate our healing journeys together, we grow not just individually but collectively. We learn from each other's experiences, gain new insights, and develop a deeper understanding of ourselves and our relationships. This growth is a testament to the transformative power of friendship. It shows us that through love, support, and shared experiences, we can overcome even the greatest challenges. Healing becomes not just an end goal but a continuous process of becoming our best selves, enriched by the connections we cherish.

As you close this book, I encourage you to take the lessons and inspiration you've found here and apply them to your own life. Reach out to your friends, nurture your relationships, and be open to new connections. Embrace vulnerability, be present, and offer encouragement and support to those around you. Remember, you have the power to be a beacon of light and hope for your friends, just as they can be for you. Together, you can create a tapestry of love and healing that enriches all your lives.

Healing with friends is a journey of love, compassion, and mutual support. It is a journey that transforms us, strengthens us, and reminds us of the profound beauty of human connection. As you continue on your path, know that you are never alone. Your friends (the ones you have and the ones that are on the way) are there with you, sharing your joys, lifting you in your sorrows, and walking beside you every step of the way. Embrace the healing power of friendship, and let it guide you toward a future filled with hope, joy, and peace. You are capable of great love and resilience, and with your friends by your side, there is no limit to what you can achieve.

Let me pray for you.

Heavenly Father, I come before You today with a heart full of hope and a desire for healing. I lift up my dear sister in Christ who is seeking to find solace, strength, and restoration within the loving embrace of a supportive community. You created us for connection and fellowship, and I pray that she finds the companionship and understanding she needs on her journey toward healing.

Lord, grant her the courage to open her heart to others, to share her struggles and burdens with trusted friends. Help her to embrace vulnerability, knowing that in doing so, she can find true connection and support. Surround her with people who reflect Your love, compassion, and grace, who will walk beside her with empathy and understanding. Father, I ask that You guide her to a community that will uplift and encourage her. Let her find a group of friends who will pray with her, laugh with her, and cry with her. May these friendships be rooted in Your Word and grounded in faith, offering her the spiritual nourishment that she needs to heal.

As she opens herself to new relationships, protect her heart from any hurt or disappointment. Help her to discern genuine connections and to build relationships that are based on mutual respect and love. Remind her that true healing often comes through the love and support of others, and that she is never alone in her journey.

Fill her with Your peace and assurance that she is worthy of love and friendship. May she experience the healing power of community and find joy in the shared moments of life. Let her see Your hand at work through the people You place in her path, and may her healing journey be a testimony to Your goodness and faithfulness.

In Jesus' name I pray, amen.

Love you, sis.

ACKNOWLEDGMENTS

To Jo and Lisa, thanks for being a text away to process any hard things from career to righteousness.

To Jamie, thanks for being a steady presence even in your own valley.

To Amanda, thank you for carrying me and my ministry with intention and grace.

To Belinda and Terrence, thanks for crying with me and protecting me.

To Ashley and Drew, thanks for building, fixing, and adding beauty to our home.

To Em, thanks for the wild adventures and laughs.

To Jen, thank you for being a steady resource of hope.

To Eryn, thanks for helping me fight the shame in my story.

To the BB's, thanks for being a Zoom call away.

To my HOC and Hopeful Woman girls, thanks for holding my story as I held yours.

To Stasia, thanks for reminding me to put on a crown.

To Lysa, thanks for braving this road before us and letting us stand on your shoulders.

ACKNOWLEDGMENTS

To Mykel, Titi, Eden, and Ezra, thanks for being family.

To my BURN fam, thanks for your support and love. #markedsafe

To my GC, Renovation, and TP church family, thanks for welcoming me home.

NOTES

Chapter 2: You Don't Feel Seen, Soothed, Safe, or Secure

1. To join the waiting list for this healing party, visit Tonijcollier.com/hope.
2. Curt Thompson (@curtthompsonmd), "We are all born into the world looking for someone looking for us," X, January 18, 2022, https://twitter.com/curt_thompsonmd/status/1483409010351120389, quoting Curt Thompson, *The Soul of Shame: Retelling the Stories We Believe About Ourselves* (IVP, 2015), 138.
3. Quoted in "When Children Feel Safe, Seen, & Soothed (Most of the Time), They Develop Security," Tina Payne Bryson, PHD (website), January 9, 2020, https://www.tinabryson.com/news/when-children-feel-safe-seen-amp-soothed-most-of-the-time-they-develop-security.

Chapter 3: Your Shame Keeps You Isolated

1. Curt Thompson et al., "Shining Light on Shame," *Advance*, Spring 2017, https://www.cccu.org/magazine/shining-light-shame/.
2. Lysa TerKeurst, *Forgiving What You Can't Forget: Discover*

NOTES

How to Move On, Make Peace with Painful Memories, and Create a Life That's Beautiful Again (Nelson Books, 2020), xvi.

Chapter 4: You're Afraid of Being Found

1. Jeff A. Benner, "Salvation," Ancient Hebrew Research Center, accessed January 15, 2025, https://www.ancient-hebrew.org/definition/salvation.htm.

Chapter 10: Embrace Diversity

1. "Looking for Preemptive Love," Search for Common Ground, accessed February 2, 2025, https://preemptivelove.org/blog/connection-through-a-cool-t-shirt-changes-a-life/.

Chapter 12: Remember That God Is in Control

1. Douglas McKelvey and Tiffany Holden, "Before Hosting," in *Every Moment Holy*, vol. 3, *The Work of the People* (Rabbit Room Press, 2023), 155, 158.

ABOUT THE AUTHOR

Toni Collier is a proud mama to Dylan and Sammie and the founder of an international women's organization called Broken Crayons Still Color, through which she helps women and children process brokenness and get to healing and hope. Toni is a speaker, host of the *Still Coloring* podcast, Hope Coach, and author of two books: *Brave Enough to be Broken* and her latest release, a children's book, *Broken Crayons Still Color*. Toni has had the opportunity to proudly stand on stages for North Point Community Church, Chick-fil-A, IF:Gathering, and MomCon. She is a regular guest on the women's TV program *TBN's Better Together* and YouVersion's verse of the day.

Toni kills illusions. She confronts the hard things. She believes the best way to meet life's challenges is head-on. And in this digital age of anxiety, Toni is teaching people all over the globe that you can be broken and still worthy; you can feel unqualified and still be called to do great things. She wants to help you find a way through the brokenness to live the most colorful life possible.